LIVING

WHILE

BLACK

To Misbah, Hayan, Yael and Malia
To Maman, Papa and Papa
To the gang of eight
To the ancestors
To us.

LIVING WHILE BLACK

The essential guide to
overcoming racial trauma

GUILAINE KINOUANI

EBURY
PRESS

Ebury Press, an imprint of Ebury Publishing,
20 Vauxhall Bridge Road,
London, SW1V 2SA

Ebury Press is part of the Penguin Random House group of companies
whose addresses can be found at global.penguinrandomhouse.com

Penguin
Random House
UK

First published by Ebury Press in 2021

www.penguin.co.uk

A CIP catalogue record for this book is available from the British Library

ISBN 9781529109436

Printed and bound in Great Britain by Clays Ltd, Elcograf S.p.A.

The authorised representative in the EEA is Penguin Random House Ireland,
Morrison Chambers, 32 Nassau Street, Dublin D02 YH68.

Penguin Random House is committed to a sustainable future for our business,
our readers and our planet. This book is made from Forest Stewardship
Council® certified paper.

Disclaimer: the events described in this book are based on the experiences of the author.
The anecdotes described are not based on any one specific individual but rather a
selection of composite characters drawing on the various experiences of the author.
Although occasionally a character has been given a name, this is for narrative flow
rather than because it represents just one person. Any similarities are purely
coincidental. This is because this is not a book about any one individual but about what
we can learn from them and how they shape our approach as readers to each other.
This book does not substitute medical or therapeutic attention. If you are suffering
from psychological distress, 'mental health' or medical issues, consider speaking to
your appointed doctor or mental health practitioner and follow their advice.

CONTENTS

CONTENTS

CHAPTER 8 – BLACK RESISTANCE

FINAL THOUGHTS – THRIVING WHILE BLACK

INTRODUCTION

Racism causes harm.

Harm to the body. And harm to the mind. Yet it is only in November 2020 that the American Medical Association recognised racism as an urgent threat to public health[1]. Thankfully, many of us did not wait for this penny to drop to tackle its impact. For about 15 years I have been working therapeutically with people of colour, supporting almost exclusively Black people distressed by racism and experiencing racial trauma. *Living While Black* seeks to offer the same support in book form, by presenting some of this work – the politics, personal and professional experiences that underlie my psychology and psychotherapy practice – to help us find connection, hope and empowerment.

Before we begin, I want to tell you a little bit about the journey to bringing this book to life. I have carved my practice out of the whiteness of psychology and of psychotherapy[2]. I have carved it out of the thousands of micro and macro experiences of discrimination and Othering I had to navigate. I have refused to ignore this rich data, the intellectual gifts contained therein and its potential to help others heal. Exploring and reflecting on my own lived experience, my lived evidence, has been central to understanding patterns of harm and domination, but also patterns of resistance. My scholarship was born out of the documentation of these patterns on Race Reflections, a platform that started as a blog and turned into a social enterprise dedicated to tackling inequality, injustice and oppression. Women – especially Black women – are socialised to distrust what we know and to be suspicious of our own authority. Oftentimes, we stop ourselves from using our gifts or we wait for someone to give us the go-ahead or to tell us how to start. And when to start. I had little support when I decided to set up my practice. What drove me was simply a strong will or perhaps a strong need to have a space where as a Black woman, a mental health professional and psychologist, I could engage with both subjects from the vantage point of being a Black female body in the world, with the richness, complexities and baggage that this entails.

Distilling these complex learnings, the primary aim of *Living While Black* is to make many of us who often haven't felt this way feel heard, seen and held. The book seeks to help Black people to thrive by first confronting the nuances of Blackness, then creating a tailored self-care plan. The first aspect is achieved via case studies, research and strategies borne out of countless hours of clinical practice and personal reflections, some of it extracted from the work of Race Reflections. The second aspect guides the reader as they self-reflect and prompts them to engage in self-care activities. *Living While Black* is a vital psychology guide for Black people. It is also an anti-racist text for others who simply want to better understand the effects of anti-Black racism so they can do better. It is also a resource for mental health, social care and medical practitioners working with Black people.

The book sheds a light on the trauma of racism – its impact on both our mental and physical health and its consequences across individuals' lifespans, across generations and across social contexts. It exposes anti-Black experiences, which society tells us are not occurring or, if they are, are not causing us harm. I want there to be no doubt that racism harms and that racial trauma is real. But equally, I want to show that it is possible to resist and to practise radical self-care while navigating white supremacy.

The material you will encounter in the book does not reach most psychology and psychotherapy 'teaching' or our collective consciousness. In fact, it is material we have learnt to censor. It is therefore rich and heavy material that you are asked to engage with and to honour. Here, you will encounter intersectional violence, intergenerational wounds, normalised trauma, everyday resistance, cultural homelessness and structural inequality and all the intersections of the socio-economic, the political, the historical, the institutional, the relational and the psychological. This is the stuff that tends not to reach Black people who seek support for psychological distress. Many mental health professionals still believe politics belong outside of our therapy rooms. That therapy is not political. The whiteness of this position is still to be accepted as a fact, let alone as a problem. Way too many mental health professionals consider social structures and indeed racism to be a distraction from the real issues or a vehicle to the real issues. And for way too many psychotherapists and psychologists the real issues still lie in our relationship with our mother (imagine a slave in distress at their condition, being asked to reflect on their relationship with their mother, to get to the 'real issues').

Over the years, Black people have come to my practice after having been further harmed by those whose job it is to facilitate healing. Psychotherapy and mental health services continue to struggle to work with racism; in fact it often reproduces it. Mindlessly. The reality is this: if you are Black and those you seek support from are unwilling to look at racism and the trauma it inflicts, these individuals or systems are simply unwilling to look you in the eye. They do not want to see you. They are not prepared to engage with the weight and complexities of our shared and often bloodied history. From there, there is usually nowhere to go but an impasse. A wall. The wall of whiteness. It is this absence that creates the gap that continues to make racism near impossible to address in therapy for way too many.

It is in that gap that some of us are forced to sit while being encouraged to displace Black rage towards our mothers because their capacity to be mothers was affected by the unjust structures within which they mothered us: the abject xenophobia, the racism, the patriarchy, the poverty. I think of my own mum too. Her back is pretty much broken. The social symbolism of a Black woman with a broken back is such a powerful one. So many of the first-generation migrant women I know have broken backs. Being the mules of society carries such a heavy price. And so many of their daughters have sore throats or are losing their voices trying to speak words few are prepared to hear. This is what being silenced can do. Black backs have a long history of carrying loads – white loads. And of being flogged for not keeping silent. But we are entitled to take some of the weight off and share it. And we are entitled to speak. And we are entitled to write. In fact, we absolutely must make our voices heard by any means necessary, if we are to stand any chance of stopping history from becoming fatality by repetition.

Living While Black is structured in eight chapters, all of which contain an analysis of societal dynamics and offer tools for the reader to support themselves and reflect on their own experiences and relationships. The book is organised as follows (you can find keyword definitions in the glossary, and in **bold**):

Chapter 1, **Being Black**, is an exploration of what being racialised as Black means. It offers the context for today's societal dynamics and inequality from my own lived experience.

Chapter 2, **Black Minds**, looks at how Black people fare in mental health institutions. It examines racial trauma and unpacks the mental health consequences of living within white supremacy.

Chapter 3, **Black Shame,** examines shame, a core consequence of racial trauma. It links this shame to racial injustice and to issues of belonging and 'homelessness'.

Chapter 4, **Black Bodies**, links the history of mistreatment of Black people via imperial and colonial violence to everyday acts of Othering. Further, it considers their impact on our body.

Chapter 5, **Raising Black Children**, focuses on the unique challenges of having a Black child or being a Black parent. It offers prompts for strengthening attachment and mitigating the intergenerational impact of racial trauma.

Chapter 6, **Working While Black**, analyses the dynamics that Black people often face in workplaces. It contextualises them historically and offers tools for navigating hostile workplace environments.

Chapter 7, **Black Love,** explores romance and intimacy and their dynamics in the context of white supremacy. It encourages reflection to help foster more authentic and fulfilling intimate relationships.

Chapter 8, **Black Resistance**, offers a roadmap for resistance, drawing on historical examples of rebellion and insurgency. It provides evidence-based tools to help you thrive as you resist white supremacy.

In **Your Radical Self-Care Plan**, you will find an action plan with various activities selected to help you connect to your ancestry, your community, your history and to nurture your body, your mind and your soul. The book also provides more specific tools to help you with specific challenges such as managing race-based stress, coping with Black shame and talking to Black children about race.

The book's title comes from an expression that has been part of the racial discourse for decades. The phrase '. . . While Black' is used by Black academics, journalists, writers and activists in the US and outside to describe the challenges of existing, resisting and thriving within white supremacy. A 1999 Minnesota Law Review paper by David A. Harris links its origins back to 'Driving While Black' – the research exposed the treatment of Black motorists by the police in 1990s America. The phrase has since been used in a variety of other contexts, such as 'Birding While Black', 'Travelling While Black' or 'Working While Black'. It highlights the differing experiences and outcomes of these mundane activities when they are carried out by Black people, because of racism, racial profiling and the associated risks to our safety; all of which will be explored in this book.

A note on research: The most reliable evidence we have when it comes to Blackness and (mental) health originates from the UK and the US. Inevitably, the research *Living While Black* is based on often comes from these countries. Still, I am a French woman with roots firmly located in Africa, so I attempt to keep my outlook on the whole diaspora.

Please also note that the contents of *Living While Black* may sometimes be distressing. You may feel a temptation to disconnect, to put the book down. We know that human beings go to extraordinary lengths to avoid pain, discomfort and tension. This has resulted in us continuing to refuse to confront the reality of racism. But breaking silences matters. It is always the first step in breaking the cycle of abuse. And we can only break silences if people accept the invitation to hear and see. Here, you are invited. While I primarily address the Black reader directly and the activities and strategies are focused on our needs, many of the tools will no doubt be helpful to others who experience racism and oppression. I want to again be clear, however, that everyone is invited to read the book. Everyone is invited to come in and reflect on the work we all must do, and think of what they themselves can do, to lighten the load.

Consider this invitation a gift.

CENTRING BLACKNESS

Living While Black unapologetically centres the experience of people racialised as Black. 'Racialisation' here is about turning certain human beings into 'Black' humans. More generally, it is the processes by which a group of people becomes defined by their race. Racialisation imposes racial meaning onto previously racially 'neutral' identities in order to reproduce the racial social order[1]. The belief that humans can be divided into different biological races, characterised by different traits and attributes, came with the commodification of Black people and the expansion of capitalism[2]. Race is a social and historical fabrication or 'construct' linked to colonial and imperial ways of viewing and organising the world[3].

We may say the (social) construction or fabrication of race is the very foundation of racism[4]. But while race is a figment of our imagination, racism is not. Here lies our first contradiction. For our purpose, we'll define racism as a system in which white groups, and those adjacent to the former, are placed in a position of power over various other races deemed inferior, and where power is used to maintain privileged access to material resources[5]. The myth of race allows resources to be allocated in ways that privilege white people and thus maintain and legitimise this fantasised racial hierarchy, which of course locates Black people as the ultimate Other, at the very bottom. It is that location in the hierarchy that leads to specific patterns of poor and violent treatment commonly referred to as **anti-Blackness.**

The term 'Black' remains controversial even among people racialised as Black people even though we are rarely asked what we think about being routinely identified as such. Some of us despise it. The historical load it carries is heavy. Still, we do know that it has been reclaimed at various points in history. Presently, this seems to be the case, as evidenced by the global phenomenon of Black Lives Matter, the slogan and movement sparked by anti-Black police brutality. In November 2020, I carried out some research. I wanted to better understand how we relate to the term 'Black'. 725 respondents racialised as Black based in the UK, US and Europe completed an online survey. A whopping 94% said they routinely identified as Black. Despite this, 59% still believed that Blackness was an identity imposed on them by society. Opposition to the term was based on its homogenising nature, its racist associations and the fact that it erased specific cultural heritage. 78% of the participants agreed that Blackness was a marker of African ancestry.

BLACKNESS AS A BLACK QUEST

Flattening some of the differences that exist within and between different Black groups is a major drawback when theorising on Blackness. And so, the task of *Living While Black* is a tough one. It is undoubtedly the case that Blackness covers a huge range of ethnic and cultural groups that are heterogenous and have various histories, ethnicities and **geopolitical** positioning. However, the search for a global connection, for commonalities in experiences and for a shared fate must be balanced out against the risk of dilution of important contextual differences.

Some may say it is an impossible task and perhaps it is. Still, the politics that inform *Living While Black* and its ethos are diasporic and **pan-Africanist.** They seek to shed light on challenges we face, because of what we share: the melanin in our skin, or even the shape of our bodies, the breadth of our noses, the thickness of our lips, the kinkiness of our hair, which cumulatively or singularly say 'Africa' to the world. Say 'primitive' to the world. Say 'inferior' to the world. Say 'dangerous' to the world. Say 'disgusting' to the world.

It is primarily this physicality that is used to racialise us, to render our body Black, to Blacken it. With white lies. It is this physicality that remains imprisoned by colonial and imperial fantasies and creates some shared experiences among all contextual differences. It is this physicality that carries within it histories of mass atrocities, histories of exploitation, histories of Othering. Histories of silencing. This is what racialisation is all about. Of course, the Black body is a body that is or is not gendered. A body that expresses itself through its sexuality and through whom it loves. A body located within a social class system. A body that through birth or geopolitical location can or cannot travel. A body that is or is not disabled. A body that sometimes sits at the intersections of all these systems and many more. Perhaps Blackness is a Black quest. But even if that is all it is, it is worth pursuing.

'Black' VERSUS 'black'

There have been ongoing debates concerning the capitalisation of 'Black' and various arguments for and against that go from the linguistic to the political[6]. In *Living While Black*, I have opted to capitalise it. This is first in recognition that the term refers to people with a shared history and ancestry traceable to Africa, however distant. Secondly and more importantly and arguably paradoxically, the capitalisation seeks to acknowledge that millions of people through the transatlantic slave trade were stripped of national and cultural ties and thus of that ancestral home. This displacement has resulted in the creation of a cultural and psychological home in Blackness that for many is now independent from Africa. This new home, regardless of our individual views and positions, deserves respect and honouring.

CHAPTER 1
BEING BLACK

DISCOVERING ANTI-BLACKNESS

I was four or five when I discovered racism[1].

I had been playing with my sister and some of the kids from the neighbourhood in front of our Parisian *banlieue* tower block, as was customary for poorer families during school holidays or weekends. There were quite a few of us, 15 or perhaps even more. Children of all backgrounds having fun, skipping, running around, and laughing the summer afternoon away. All of us still quite oblivious to the dire social deprivation we were accustomed to and the hostility created by our existence in France. A white man erupted from a ground floor flat in the tower, shouting, clearly aggrieved by the noise we were collectively making. After his rant, he ran directly towards my elder sister and pushed her from behind.

She was six or seven at the most. The white man pushed her so violently that she was propelled forward, fell, and scraped the ground for a few metres. Once immobile, much of the skin at the back of her arms had gone. Some of the children quickly ran to our second floor flat to alert my parents. Moments later my mother appeared downstairs to find my sister, other children and me in tears and my sister covered in blood. Within minutes she was at the assailant's door, furious and demanding an explanation. She was greeted by a barrage of racist abuse, including the N-word of course.

Rant over, the man proceeded to punch her in the face so forcefully her skin turned blue-black, one of her eyes became red with blood and half her face swelled up.

This was not a half-hearted attack. It was a determined, unrestrained, chest out, full force, knock-out hit. The kind of punch a charged-up and angry man throws at an enemy assessed to be of considerable force. The kind of heavyweight punch that is full of hatred and carries the weight of the history of terror. Of white terror. The kind of punch no woman should ever have to bear. But that Black women often do. I do not remember much after the punch. Things have blurred in my memory, but I can still see my mother standing after the assault. Standing tall, defiant and in dignified silence. Not a single tear. Not a word in retort. Although I do not remember this, I am told the white man was arrested minutes later, knife in hand, threatening to kill her in front of a full audience of distraught children. Imagine the scene. The loudness, the chaos, the screams, the powerlessness.

SCHOOLING WHILE BLACK

Later, I was exposed to a different kind of racism when my mother got into a dispute with my primary school[2]. Being born in February and as a result missing the official cut-off point for admission by a few days or so, the decision as to whether I could start or not was at the discretion of the school. While for white children, starting school a little early was rarely an issue, the school took umbrage that my mother thought her child was ready to start school. My entry was barred – a rare occurrence. My mother challenged the school. Mainly out of principle, as she knew she and I were being treated differently. The school dug their heels in and decided that the only way to prove I was sufficiently intelligent – or 'cognitively ready' – was to test my IQ, seeming almost certain that I would not overcome this hurdle. I was subjected to a battery of tests by a team of psychologists. Then, they wrote their report. The school's own appointed psychologists had found I had a much higher 'intelligence' than average and was, in fact, advanced for my age. Reluctantly, I was allowed in.

Fast-forward to my teens. During a philosophy class, I questioned Descartes' **dualism**. The teacher responded by calling me a monkey who was incapable of thinking and was, instead, looking at the finger of Descartes, as Descartes was pointing to the sun. Then, in high school, I had a history and geography teacher who taught us all about the important job France did in civilising and enlightening Africa from the Dark Ages, as part of a module on **colonialism**. The course was so whitewashed, uncritical and steeped in white nostalgia, it was psychologically violent. In the end, students of colour were excused, off the record, from attending this class. A compromise to avoid the disturbance of our questions and critical eyes, or to have to rethink the curriculum.

Throughout my teens I watched my mother continue to battle white teachers' low and stereotypical expectations. None of us had 'what it took' to go to university. Against all 'odds' and our 'limited' intellectual capabilities, we count among ourselves as siblings: one physicist, two economists, one accountant and – wow – a psychologist. That would be me. Seven out of eight of us did go to university, and most of us obtained postgraduate qualifications. For my part, I studied English at La Sorbonne in Paris straight after my baccalaureate. As part of an American civilisation class, we were taught that the US was the number one economic power in the world due to its high national IQ, but that as a nation it was still being held back because of the low IQ of African Americans.

WHITE WOMEN AND LIBERAL RACISM

Afterwards, I found myself studying psychology in Britain. There I encountered a different kind of racism. One I was ill-equipped to deal with or understand. The liberal kind. Insidious, normalised and shifty. The kind of racism middle-class white women excel at[3]. The kind of racism that hides even from the mind and body that harbours it. It hides behind decorum, impeccable manners and professionalism. Professional racism, we may say. The kind of racism that knows better than you and constantly rationalises itself away, weaponising innocence and good intentions.

I learnt what white women as a group can and do get away with within white institutions. Whenever I reflect on these times, it is the faces of white middle-class women I see. Smiling. I learnt that society will not recognise racist violence if it is not obvious. If it is not a white man pushing you from behind or punching you in the face. I learnt that hurting the egos of middle-class professional white women, by asking them to reflect on their racism, is one of the most treacherous things a Black woman can do. I learnt that equality and diversity policies are primarily used to hide racism and often to protect institutions from their racism. My years in academic psychology have, beyond the shadow of a doubt, been the most distressing years of my adult life. I somehow survived; in fact, I did much more than survive: I thrived. I too, still stand, dignified. But not silent. There are various ways to resist.

ON WRITING MYSELF IN

I have thought long and hard about whether I should write myself into the book that I am writing. I am a therapist, but therapy is political. The violent structures within which I exist and do therapy, and the experiences you will be introduced to later in the book, are not separate from my life or yours – whether you know it or not. Or like it or not. We are part of the world we write about; the world we write about lives inside us.

Too often Black people are told directly or indirectly that we must keep quiet when we experience racial injustices – that is if these experiences are even recognised as racial injustices[4]. We are told that if we are upset about racist experiences, that is if they are accepted as racist experiences, that there is never anything to be distressed about. If we ever get distressed, we are reminded that we must be more resilient. More robust. More moved on. More mature. Speak not, we are told, but if you must speak, speak gently. Cry not, but if you must cry, cry silently. Write not, but if you must write, write impersonally. Exist not, but if you must exist, be as invisible as you can be. Take up as little space as you can take. Let us not see you, let us not hear you, and let us forget you exist because your existence reminds us of who we are.

THE ROOTS OF OUR RESISTANCE

We owe so much of our spirit of survival and resistance to our foremothers, famous and anonymous alike. Those who have struggled in the cotton or sugar cane fields of 'new worlds' and those who have fought for independence from colonialism. But also, all the others who have bowed their heads, scrubbed, and sacrificed their dignity and at times their health to give us the best chances in life. Those who have carried white bodies on their back as carers while being spat at so that we could get a chance at having an education. Often the same who just decades later were shipped back like unwanted cargo caught up in the Windrush debacle and the so-called hostile environment, as though they had known any other kind of environment in Britain. Their dignity and resilience, their beauty, we must never forget. The gifts they have left us will forever be with us.

So, what I know is the sum of where I have walked, where I stand in the world and what I have learnt as a therapist. However, the multi-generational histories that birthed me have birthed this book too. French people sometimes call people like me, these reported 'second generation of migrants', *les déracinés* or those who are uprooted. Trees pulled out from their roots. Trees, it is therefore assumed, without a firm foundation and no grounding. But our roots are more solid than they appear. They simply extend beyond the boundaries of one nation. They branched out from and into various countries and cultures. But the further away from the soil a tree is, the thicker and stronger the roots need to be for its branches to survive and flourish. It is France that has sought to uproot us from our Frenchness.

In the same way, so many Black people in the UK and throughout the world are reminded of their Otherness by being constantly asked: 'where are you really from?' in white spaces. The assumption, of course, being that they do not belong or, at least that they do not belong 'here'. That their home is elsewhere. No one subjected to chronic experiences of racism in their homeland can ever fully feel at home in their home. Particularly, when these Othering experiences occur in their tender years and are repeated throughout their entire life. But it is where the story starts.

'I CAN'T BREATHE!'

Have you ever tried to swallow your cries? This is what imposed silences feel like. Racism makes breathing laborious. It makes it hard to breathe. On the 25 May 2020, George Floyd, an African American man, was arrested on suspicion of attempting to buy a pack of cigarettes with a counterfeit 20-dollar bill. He was publicly suffocated to death by Derek Chauvin, a white police officer. The arrest was filmed by a witness, showing Chauvin kneeling on Floyd's neck for over eight minutes while handcuffed and face down on the ground. Seeing death approaching, Floyd repeatedly pleaded for his life[5]: 'I can't breathe', 'they will kill me'. The world watched in horror as his prediction came true. He was killed on the streets and in plain sight. Some might say, like a dog. The death of Floyd hit the world hard. It turned into a catalyst for global protests[6], demonstrations against anti-Black police brutality and demands for racial justice and the abolition of the police. However, the murder of George Floyd did more than trigger unrest and street disturbances. It created real collective distress and despair among Black people in the US and well beyond[7].

The trauma of racism was laid bare for us all to see. Anger and sadness combined forces. Calls for changes in policing, accountability and complete social reformation swept many Western nations. All with their own histories of anti-Black police murders. Along with the name of George Floyd, the names of others resonated in the streets. Justice for Trayvon Martin. Justice for Eric Gardner. Justice for Sandra Bland. Justice for Breonna Taylor! The name of Adama Traoré was screamed on the streets of France together with other names that started to be called in my childhood such as the name Makomé M'Bowolé. In the UK, Olaseni Lewis, Sheku Bayoh, Kingsley Burrell, Rashan Charles, Sean Rigg, Roger Sylvester, Joy Gardner and Cynthia Jarrett and so many more who were suffocated to death or died after contact with the police or other statutory services. So many names. Too many to attempt to recall here.

Tears, screams and direct action englobed so many nations. Black Lives Matter appeared on placards. Message after message of angst reached my mailbox: 'I can't stop crying'; 'I have not slept in days'; 'how do I prepare my children for this?'; 'I am exhausted' and; 'I do not know how to talk to my white friends about Living While Black'. Each email hit me right in the heart. Holding on to hope can sometimes feel impossible. It is so easy to feel as though one is one step away from falling into the depths of madness or despair while being expected to keep it all under wraps. Writing, and especially writing myself in, is my act of protest. **Anti-Blackness** is not an academic project. We live our theories, but our lives are not theoretical. We are all involved here, so we must connect. We must connect the dots. And again, we must simply connect.

Over the years, I have learnt too that each time I dig deep into my own experience, unpack it, explore it, bear witness to it, by putting it into words, somebody – often several people – miles and miles away, thanks me for writing about *them*. For making their story known. The more intricate the details, the more of myself I give, the more strangers, complete strangers, say they see themselves in my words. Writing and reading is simply not enough if we keep ourselves at the head or cerebral level.

CONNECTING AS AN ACT OF LOVE

There is something powerfully humanising in those connections that writing with honesty brings, that writing and reading with an open heart creates. I think ultimately connecting with our experiences allows us to connect with the experience of others and for others to connect with theirs and so forth. Understanding the lived experience of one single individual gets us much closer than anything else to grasping the global phenomenon and machinery that is racism. Therefore, stories of survival, of defiance, of resistance allow us all to better understand hate but also to better understand love. Out of this connection is born a recognition of our shared humanity, a powerful antidote to oppression, if one does accept the invitation.

We have worked hard in our society to make love irrelevant and obsolete within mainstream social justice work and politics. And to make social justice and politics irrelevant to psychology and mental health. There is often an implicit contempt for matters of the heart. We have become suspicious of human feelings, arguably for good reasons. However, without transparently sharing the struggles and the triumphs of our lives, there cannot be understanding. Without transparency, there cannot be a connection. Connection between the reader's world and the words of the author.

Interconnectedness is therefore a shared fate. I believe that every text is in some way autobiographical, whether openly or not. Who we are, even if only in traces, is always in there, present in between the words.

My position, as I hope will become clearer in the rest of the book, is that connection matters. And while connection matters, love matters even more. And conversely, without connection, there can be no love. Love for the self but also love for the Other. Touching hearts is no guaranteed way to radical social transformation, but it is part of the revolution. It is no coincidence that white groups go to extraordinary lengths to avoid being touched. And one way to avoid being

touched is to be oblivious to the realities and lived experiences of racism. To erase them from the collective mind. To
normalise wilful amnesia. To constantly reconfigure one's
memory to set it free of the violence and suffering that is all
around us. Suffering that would again otherwise force that
human connection. Connection, therefore, makes detachment, dissociation and complicity much more difficult. It is
harder to shoot someone in the face – literally and figuratively –
while staring into their eyes.

So, this transparency is first intended to help you contextualise the issues raised in the book and to grasp why it is
being written. It is to help the Black reader know they are not
alone. Then, it is to connect our lived experience to **anti-
racism**, or the act of actively seeking to dismantle or combat
racism – and to love. A deep love for Black people and any-
body else who is oppressed around the world underscores
this project. But also, perhaps, an unconscious desire to pro-
voke love in those who do us harm, perhaps despite
themselves. This love aspiration is not naïve, romantic or
immature. Nor is it the kind of love that often requires that
Black people and those harmed by racism should forever
turn the other cheek. No, it is the kind of love that is political.
A Black feminist kind of love. The love I am talking about is a
militant one. One that cannot be separated from justice, or a
desire to repair and rebuild a fairer world. A love that requires
being there and showing up. A love that is all about daring to
see the other in their full humanity. A love that invokes
compassion. Without compassion, we cannot hope to be
motivated enough to change. We cannot hope to hope.

bell hooks[8] defines this love as 'a combination of care,
knowledge, responsibility, respect, trust, and commitment'.
Perhaps it *is* possible to force change. No revolution was ever
built on love alone, no matter how radical. Still, sustaining
change requires more than coercion. Coercion breeds resistance and rebellion, and no one on this planet knows this
better than Black people. We cannot force connection. We
cannot legislate love. Therefore, bell hooks teaches us that

power breeds lovelessness. Anti-Blackness, we may say, is a defence against love. It is a way to avoid the intimacy and connection to the self and to others. A sophisticated and atrociously costly way to avoid seeing and being seen. I hope sharing a bit of my experience will allow you to connect to the human that I am. To humanity. And, by extension, to see the humanity of those whose bodies look like mine. Anti-Blackness is a matter of life and death. I hope that connection will help dismantle all the walls so many put around themselves to avoid being touched by us and choose life over death. I hope because we need to hope – without hope, there can be no resistance.

SUMMARY

1.
Experiences of racism for Black people are ubiquitous.
They happen across contexts and often throughout our
lifespan, they shape our life trajectories and worldview
including what we come to believe about the world, what
we're able to see in the world as well as our vocational
and/or professional interests or talents.

2.
**As a result, transparency and reflexivity are important
qualities for anyone who wants to understand race**.
Writing with honesty and integrity challenges whiteness.
It also aims to help the reader better understand the
personal context of *Living While Black* and the lived
experiences that can lead to racial trauma.

3.
**Connection is fundamental to love and to authentic
human relationships**, yet racism forces disconnection at
various levels, most fundamentally between Black people
and people who perform anti-Blackness. Anti-racism must
therefore involve building authentic connections.

4.
**It is not possible to separate the writer from where
they stand in the world, in the same way that it is not
possible to separate the mind from the body.** As we will
see in the chapters to come, reconnecting mind, body
and soul is central to healing from racial trauma.

In the next chapter, **BLACK MINDS**, we consider the
institutional context and inequalities in relation to Black
mental health and look at the various ways we can
understand racial trauma.

RACE REFLECTIONS

You have learnt about the personal context of *Living While Black*, including my experience of racial injustice and how it influences my worldview and work on racism. This section gives you the opportunity to reflect on your own personal context and develop reflective skills. These are needed not only to engage with the current chapter, but also to prepare you for the rest of the book.

Gearing yourself towards self-care

Engaging with racism and injustice is a risk factor for psychological distress. For this reason, it is vital that, as you go through the book, you actively seek to take care of your body, your mind and your soul by engaging in self-care. I define it as the deliberate steps we take to practise self-protection, self-nurture, self-soothing and self-kindness. Please reflect on what the definition evokes in you and the kinds of activities you could engage in to fulfil all elements of the definition. Then ask yourself this question: what do you need to maintain a sense of hope?

....

....

....

....

....

What have you learnt from this chapter that you have found most challenging?

You may want to explore the physical responses, images and thoughts that came to you and explore what they might take you back to. Please use the Race Reflections reflective model (p.207) to help you.

....

....

....

....

....

When was your first encounter with racism?

*What were the circumstances and how old were you? Try to remind yourself of as much detail as possible. Connect to the feelings you felt at the time. Name them. As you connect, it is helpful to become attuned to how your body responds to these racialised memories. Many will be **embodied**; treat this as data and be curious about them. What can they teach you about racial injustice? Could they help you recognise racism? What do they tell you about self-care?*

....

....

....

....

....

Reflect on your identity development

__Racial identity development__ concerns our growing sense of belonging or identification with a racial group, here Blackness. It typically occurs in early adolescence and when we go from a place of racial obliviousness to, we could say, racial consciousness. The box overleaf summarises Cross's model. Dr Cross is an American scholar and researcher on racial identity. Please review the stages and consider what stage you may be at and what events and actions you may use to support your position.

....

....

....

....

....

Racial Identity Development

Cross's 5 Stages of Black Racial Identity Development:

- Stage 1 – Pre-encounter: 'it is better to be white'.

- Stage 2 – Encounter: forced acknowledgement of racism.

- Stage 3 – Immersion/Emersion: active avoidance of 'symbols' of whiteness.

- Stage 4 – Internalization: connected to Black peers; willing to engage with Whites.

- Stage 5 – Internalization-Commitment: personal sense of what it means to be Black; commitment to the welfare of Blacks as a whole; comfortable interacting with Whites; positive racial identity.

Credit: William E. Cross, Jr. Cross, W. (1991). *Shades of Black: Diversity in African American Identity*. Philadelphia: Temple University Press.

ACTION POINT
GET A REFLECTIVE JOURNAL

You are encouraged to keep a reflective journal throughout your engagement with *Living While Black* and ideally after. Your reflective journal is where you will record your thoughts and reactions. If you do not feel that writing is the best way to engage in your learning, feel free to use an alternative way to record your thoughts, feelings and reflections (including embodied responses). Your first action is simply to secure such a journal.

CHAPTER 2

BLACK MINDS

As human beings we are designed to feel safe, and to feel like we belong. Therefore, we can never really get used to or become fully desensitised to racism, however hard we may try. We often simply end up succeeding at denying, burying or dissociating from the pain it causes. In this chapter we consider the institutional context of **Black mental health**. We look at well-documented inequalities, but we also go much further. We consider the 'Black experience' when it comes to mental health systems. An experience that sits at the intersection of various systems of oppression.

BLACK MINDS, WHITE INSTITUTIONS

Case study: Mike
Mike is a young Black man who has spent his life in London after coming to England to seek asylum due to war in his country of origin. Growing up, Mike hated school. Whenever trouble occurred, teachers usually assumed he was responsible. Mike felt treated as though he was not expected to do well, unlike other children. He eventually believed he was not as clever as the other students and began to feel out of place in school. In his early teens, Mike started avoiding school and truanting, which resulted in him getting expelled. His white peers were given warnings for similar infractions. To fill his days, Mike spent much time on the streets of London. At about 17, he experimented with cannabis.

*Shortly after, he started 'hearing voices' and was first diagnosed with '**Drug Induced Psychosis**', then with schizophrenia and was compulsorily detained under the **Mental Health Act (1983)**. Mike noticed many other Black men in the hospital and resented being there. Many of these other Black men had been detained in mental health services following the involvement of the police. Very few Black men were in therapy or were given the chance to talk about their lived experience. When racism was broached, staff often changed the subject or became defensive. Mike had to endure racial slurs on the ward, mainly from other mental health service users. Mike remained in hospital for about a month. Weeks after his discharge, he got into a confrontation with the police. He claimed to have been stopped by the police three times in the same day. He also reported having been stopped the day before. Mike had recurrently seen police officers target other Black kids for searches. He became defiant and angry and refused to comply. The situation escalated and Mike ended up being physically restrained by three officers. He was arrested and eventually charged with common assault. In court, no one seemed interested in his experience with the police or with schools. Instead, he was deemed to have a problem with authority and sentenced to six months in prison, where he became unwell again. There, he was transferred to a **Medium Secure Unit**, which is a mental health service providing treatment for those who have been arrested or committed a crime and who are diagnosed with psychiatric disorders. And, they are deemed to pose high risks of harm to themselves or others. He was compulsorily detained for several years in the Medium Secure Unit. It is there that I met him, and we started doing some therapeutic work.*

Over the years, I have worked with several young men with similar stories to Mike's. The bulk of this work focused on helping these young men unpack their experience of racism, rebuild trust (including towards themselves) and process their anger. This story speaks to the multitude of inequalities and violence Black people often experience when dealing with mental health services. It also reveals the layers of trauma that can co-exist within a single individual. Here, the trauma of war, of abuse and of structural racism, all lead to an extraordinarily complex picture when it comes to Black mental health.

In our quest to understand the challenges Black people experience with our mental health services and the apparent excess of '**mental health problems**' in our communities, we must remember challenges exist in relation to these conceptualisations. The Eurocentricity and failure to consider the historical and socio-political realities of Blackness has been the cause of criticism for decades. Wherever possible I prefer to use the terms 'distress', 'psychological distress' or 'suffering' when considering the 'Black experience'. This is to avoid being limited to a medical framework of understanding our experiences or to individualistic lenses. However, when drawing on findings from the existing literature, medical terminology cannot be avoided entirely as the **medical model** is still the dominant one to understand psychological suffering in the West.

Our definitions of mental health will vary from person to person. However, generally when we talk about mental health we are talking about our subjective sense of wellbeing and when we talk about 'mental health problems', we are referring to difficulties in relating to ourselves, others and/or to the world. Or, we refer to feelings, thoughts and behaviours that have adverse effects on our ability to lead fulfilling lives. (Again, these definitions are not without problems and we will return to them later in the chapter.)

When it comes to mental health, stark inequalities exist across racial lines. To assess them, the Department of Health (DoH) has historically considered three main classes[1] of inequality across racial groups:

1. Inequality in terms of access or in the route different racial groups take to access support.
2. Inequality in terms of experience or how various groups experience mental health services.

3. Inequality in terms of outcomes that are centred on what happens to us clinically once we get into services, such as whether we 'recover' and go on to live fulfilling lives or whether we end up being 'revolving door patients'.

The inequitable treatment of Black people has been documented at all three levels. The list of mental health inequality is long and seriously disturbing.

To summarise, Black groups are subject to more adverse and coercive mental health practices than any other ethnic group in the UK. We are more likely to:

- Get mental health care and treatment by force such as through the involvement of the police[2].
- Be detained within psychiatric hospitals against our will[3].
- Be assessed or stereotyped as dangerous more than any other group in the UK and less likely to be offered psychotherapy.
- Spend years in and out of mental health institutions and to be over-medicated[4].
- Be diagnosed with having a severe and enduring mental health problem[5] such as psychosis more than both white and Asian groups.
- Not to receive support for 'common mental health problem' (e.g. anxiety and depression), yet just as likely to experience them.

We still experience racism within mental health services and are often reluctant to engage with them, which leads to cycles of coercion, fear and stigma.

The picture does not appear much more favourable in the US. Although it has been acknowledged that Black people are much less likely than white groups to be the recipients of mental health support despite their needs[6].

In the US:

- Black groups are less likely to seek mental health support than other racial groups[7].
- Although African Americans may overall be less likely to experience 'depression', when depressed it is more likely that their condition will be chronic and that they will suffer higher levels of disability compared with whites[8].
- African-Americans with severe depression are more likely to be misdiagnosed as having schizophrenia, likely due to racial bias and racism[9,10].
- Like in the UK, one of the most consistent race inequalities is the disproportionately high rate of psychotic diagnoses among African Americans despite the lack of evidence for biological predisposition[11,12].
- Alarmingly, the suicide rate of Black children is on the up, the only group where the rate is growing[13,14].

These inequities are concerning enough as they are, but they do not end here. We, as a group, are also more likely to die within mental health institutions. This context laid the foundation for the death of David 'Rocky' Bennett.

Case study: Rocky
*In 1998, mental health patient David 'Rocky' Bennett, a Black Rastafarian man, was killed while physically restrained on a psychiatric ward. This death had a seismic cultural impact for those in the mental health system. The independent inquiry found that David had died as a direct result of prolonged face-down physical restraint and because of the amount of force used by five members of staff. David had been restrained, again, face-down, on the floor for 25 minutes. Restrained in what is called a '**prone position**'. A position only to be used for the shortest of instances*

to minimise the risk of injury or death. Three minutes was eventually recommended by the inquiry[12].

The inquiry into David's death found a catalogue of failings including the stereotyping of David. It also showed that there was no real attempt to engage with his family as part of the treatment of his 'psychosis' diagnosis during a period of almost 20 years. David was repeatedly treated as 'a nuisance to be contained' by over-medication. His cultural, social and religious needs were not considered when viewing his reactions and experiences on the ward. David had suffered from racist abuse throughout his stay in the hospital. But as staff were unaware of the 'corrosive and cumulative effect of racist abuse upon a Black patient', David was not offered support. In fact, his complaints were often not even recorded. David's race-based distress was ignored until his death.

Over the years, I have pictured David 'Rocky' Bennett's last moments in my head. The findings of the inquiry were published around the time I was starting up as a mental health professional. I have repeatedly imagined what the scene might have been like as he lay on the floor as his life slipping away. I imagined him thrashing about trying to break free. I imagined him gasping for air and repeatedly pleading for his life. David was killed in a way that painfully and eerily echoes the death of George Floyd in the United States. I can easily imagine David saying, 'I can't breathe', however muffled his voice might have been. There is evidence that, like George Floyd, David was heard saying, 'they are trying to kill me'.

David Bennett's death has parallels with another Black death[15]. Today, few in the UK are unfamiliar with the death of Stephen Lawrence, the Black teenager stabbed to death in 1993 in an unprovoked racist attack[16,17]. I was not living in Britain when Stephen was murdered. But his murder is one of the first things I learnt about this country when I migrated. The poor handling of the police investigation into his murder led to delayed and only partial justice for the boy and his loved ones. The report on the public inquiry led by Sir

William Macpherson was published in 1999 and found the police force to be institutionally racist.

This sent shockwaves into the country, challenging its long-held self-image as a tolerant and racially blind liberal haven. Although the findings from the inquiry led to significant cultural changes in attitudes towards law enforcement and in community policing, the Lawrences only obtained a semblance of justice. Only two of Stephen's murderers were eventually imprisoned following a change in the **double jeopardy law**. It was after almost two decades of tireless campaigning by his parents and an unsuccessful private prosecution that in 2012 David Norris and Gary Dobson were finally convicted of murder and received life sentences. The murder of Stephen Lawrence and the subsequent botched investigation left an indelible blood stain on the nation's consciousness.

One factor that unites the deaths of David Bennett and Stephen Lawrence is statutory services' refusal to consider the centrality of racism in the tragedy that unfolded and in the deaths of these two young Black men. The refusal, overt or covert, to confront the lived reality of racism in the lives of Black people is a tell-tale sign of institutional racism. The refusal to take seriously the testimonies of those directly impacted by racism kills. Our society is still in denial about the impact of racism. And, the refusal to see racism often translates into the refusal to see us as human beings. David and Stephen were not seen in their full humanity. They never stood a chance.

Contact between the police and Black groups has become a public health concern. It has the real potential to damage the health of individuals 'stopped and searched'. Over the years I have encountered hundreds of young Black men in community, forensic and clinical settings. I can say, with no hesitation, that young Black men's experience of the police has been one of the most virulent and recurrent issues I have been presented with. Expectedly, it was often accompanied by feelings of rage, despair, helplessness, distrust and alienation. Feelings strongly associated with psychological distress.

We now have some research findings to support this clinical experience. We have limited data in the UK; however in the US greater anxiety and even trauma symptoms have been found among those 'stopped and frisked'. This distress is closely related to how intrusive contact with the police is, the number of 'stop and frisk' events reported over one's lifetime and the sense of injustice[18,19]. We also have some research that evidences that witnessing the police killing of unarmed Black Americans has predictable detrimental effects on the collective mental health of Black American adults in the general population. Researchers have called it the 'spill over' effects of police brutality[18].

Mental health inequalities have not abated. In fact, they are getting worse. There is a high proportion of Black people who have come to find death in places where they should have found solace and safety, killed by those meant to care for them. Further US data shows that people with mental health problems may be up to 16 times more likely to be killed by the police[19]. The intersections of Blackness and disability and that of Blackness and psychological distress are some of the deadliest. Imagine living in a world where psychological suffering puts you at risk of further suffering and increases the chance of you experiencing violent racism, if not death? It is a hard thought to hold.

PSYCHOTHERAPY AND RACISM

I have studied psychology for about seven years. In these years, I have never received a single lecture on racism, let alone on racial trauma. This is despite the inquiry into the death of David Bennett recommending that a better understanding of the impact of racism is central to reducing race inequalities in the mental health system, and the ongoing inequalities we have just covered.

I wrote in Chapter 1 about the risks that still exist in calling out racism and the dynamics this can set in motion; these exist in the mental health field too. White ignorance plays a massive part. And so, troublingly, in my clinical and research work I have come across the very same silencing experiences in Black patients who attempted to bring racism into their psychotherapy. Unsurprisingly, Black people's voices and lived experiences are virtually absent from the psychology and psychotherapy literature and research. The difficulty of psychology and mental health professionals in addressing and working with racism is well documented[20].

Through this absence, psychology, and more broadly mental health services[21], may be charged at best with complicity in the active reproduction of this conspiracy of silence, and at worst with facilitating psychological harm and re-traumatisation. The lack of understanding of the centrality of racism in Black people's experience of psychological distress has dire consequences. Not least, normalising abuses of power in society, thus the upholding of white supremacy. It also contributes to distrust, stigma and fear of mental health services. It feeds race inequalities within the mental health system[21]. Not treating racial trauma and racism seriously renders psychology and psychotherapy vulnerable to accusations of institutional racism. And, institutional racism is not just about 'cultural incompetence' – it is also about a continued tolerance of dehumanising practices and a systemic failure to challenge and change racially discriminatory patterns of care.[22]

DEFINING RACIAL TRAUMA

While society refuses to see racism, racism continues to harm us. There is little doubt that the lived experience of race discrimination is a significant factor in the over-prevalence of psychological distress that can be found within Black groups. It has been linked to various manifestations of psychological suffering including 'depression, psychosis, anxiety' and trauma[23,24].

But what is racial trauma? The American Psychological Association (APA)[24] refers to trauma as an 'emotional response to a terrible event like an accident, rape or natural disaster'. It further adds that long-term reactions include unpredictable emotions, flashbacks, strained relationships and even physical symptoms like headaches or nausea. Immediately after the event, shock and denial are typical.

To understand the case for racial trauma, we also need to understand '**Post-Traumatic Stress Disorder (PTSD)**'[24]. It is the trauma diagnosis *par excellence*. PTSD is a condition characterised by the re-experiencing of a traumatic event(s), hyper-vigilance or what we may refer to as alertness to possible dangers and threats, and the avoidance of reminders of the trauma.

According to the latest version of the *Diagnostic Statistical Manual*, criterion A for a diagnosis of PTSD means the traumatic event or stressor must involve exposure to death, injury or sexual violence or the threat thereof, in one of the following ways:

1. direct exposure.
2. indirect exposure (e.g. witnessing a stressor/traumatic event occurring to someone else).
3. hearing about violent/accidental event(s) someone close experienced.
4. being repeatedly exposed to graphic details of a stressor/traumatic event[25,26].

Having met criterion A, the additional criteria are essentially as follows:

- **Criterion B:** recurrently reliving the stressor/traumatic event.
- **Criterion C:** avoiding reminders of the stressor/traumatic event.

- **Criterion D:** negative change in thoughts/feelings after the stressor/traumatic event.
- **Criterion E:** experiencing trauma-related arousal and reactivity.
- **Criterion F:** the symptoms must be present for at least one month.
- **Criterion G:** evidence of distress or there must be some impairment in functioning e.g. difficulties at work/school.
- **Criterion H:** symptoms must not be caused by medication, substance use, or other illness.

Thus, broadly speaking, trauma describes responses to frightening events. It refers to a long-lasting sense of overwhelm, unsafeness and distress that follows exposure. Although we have known for decades that racism can cause traumatic responses, it is only recently that the links between race discrimination, racism and trauma have received mainstream clinical attention. Part of the case for racial trauma as a conceptual tool is that so many people distressed by racism were not meeting the diagnostic criteria for PTSD, which again currently revolves around the threat to one's life. Many clinicians have argued and found[26] empirically (via scientific research) that trauma symptoms can exist in the absence of threat to life. Even smaller and less extreme, but repeated experiences of discrimination and Othering can cumulate into significant psychological difficulties, 'psychiatric' presentations and experiences that often mirror PTSD (and other 'psychiatric disorders') 'symptoms'.

Racial trauma is therefore a framework to describe the physical and emotional responses that can follow exposure to racism, and which may, clinically speaking, include any of the 'symptoms' listed above and indeed many more. The core defining feature of racial trauma frameworks is racism and its various manifestations as the cause of psychological distress.

RACE-BASED TRAUMATIC STRESS INJURY

Race-Based Traumatic Stress Injury[27] is a framework created by Dr Robert Carter, an African American psychologist. The framework defines trauma as: the emotional pain that a person may feel after encounters with racism. According to this framework, the way in which people experience encounters with racism can vary from one individual to another. Responses are dependent on an individual's background or health, and how they make sense of what has happened to them.

A person who interprets their racial encounter as extremely negative, sudden or uncontrollable may start to show signs of stress and trauma. Carter suggests that for trauma to be present, the reaction or symptoms need to include: psychological intrusion (e.g. flashbacks), avoidance of reminders of the initial distressing event and 'arousal' (e.g. being easily startled). According to Carter, the signs of racial trauma may be exhibited emotionally, physiologically, cognitively, behaviourally, or in combination of two or more of these. One may express the trauma through anxiety, anger, rage, depression, low self-esteem, shame and guilt. Although not a 'formal' diagnosis within dominant psychiatric categorisation systems, Race-Based Traumatic Stress Injury has gained much traction as a clinical framework, particularly in the US.

A further conceptualisation of racial trauma is that of African American psychologist Dr Shelly Harrell[28]. She offers a six-level framework that examines the ways in which we are harmed by racism, through:

1. **Racism-related life events:** These are racial events such as assaults and other acts of race discrimination that target us directly and unequivocally.
   For example: When we are called a racist term or assaulted because we are Black.

2. **Vicarious racism:** Occurs when the exposure to racism is indirect.

   For example: When we hear stories of or witness racism occurring to those around us.

3. **Daily racist micro-stressors**: These are subtle, normalised and ambiguous acts of racist denigration. The kinds of acts many would refer to as **microaggressions** today.

   For example: Being followed in a store or being repeatedly asked, 'Where are you from?'.

4. **Chronic contextual stressor**: The mere awareness of structural race inequality and unequal distribution of resources. *For example:* being exposed to race inequality statistics via the media or popular culture.

5. **Collective experiences of racism**: Witnessing the racism inflicted on one's racial group. *For example:* witnessing the murder of Black people at the hands of the state.

6. **Transgenerational transmission of group trauma**: Aspects of oppression related to historical events are passed on. *For example:* when our parents share tips about surviving white supremacy.

The last three levels of Dr Harrell's framework deal with the impact of racism at group level, something that tends to evade most conversations on racism and racial trauma. They help us to understand the Black Lives Matter movement and why so many Black people around the world were so distraught by the murder of George Floyd. This framework is helpful as it highlights two important things: firstly, the chronic nature of racial trauma, which sets it apart from most other forms of trauma. Secondly, it stresses the collective harm that racism can inflict. Other frameworks exist for this purpose and we will cover these later in the book.

RACIAL TRAUMA: SIGNS AND MANIFESTATIONS

How we define racial trauma and the framework we use will invariably shape what we pay attention to when it comes to signs and manifestations, and indeed what we consider to be signs and manifestations of racial trauma. We have now examined various forms of racism, and throughout the book you will be encouraged to think well beyond the individual when conceptualising racial trauma (while still holding the individual's experience in mind). Thinking about signs and manifestations is no different. The table below presents some of the multi-level signs and manifestations of racism I have formulated:

Signs and manifestations of racial trauma

Individual level	Family level	Community level
• Distrust of white people • Shame of heritage/internalised racism • Hypervigilance/cultural paranoia • Substance misuse • Anxiety • Low mood/depression • Low self-esteem • Excessive work/perfectionism • Self-harming behaviours • Fear of speaking out/self-silencing	• Distrust of white people • Raising children to comply/work 'twice as hard' • Attachment and/or relationship difficulties • Harsh punishment/discipline of children • Child neglect and abuse • Repetition of cycles of neglect/abuse intergenerationally • Silence and difficulty naming racism • Fear a loved one may come to harm/overprotection	• Acceptance of the status quo • Learned helplessness • Identification with the aggressor • Intra-group conflicts (through displacement of aggression) • Scapegoating 'transgressors' e.g. those who don't toe the white line/keep silent • Enactment of other axes of oppression e.g. ableism, homophobia • Reproduction of historical relational scripts such as subservience • Respectability/assimilative politics

The above is not an exhaustive list. Instead, it aims to get you thinking about the multitude of ways in which racial trauma can manifest itself and be recognised. The signs will vary depending on the individual and the social context, in the same way that the impact of the same psychological stressor might look quite different in different people. How we process racist incidents, our history, past adverse events, family survival and strategies – all these factors and more intersect to create responses to racism and therefore, racial trauma presentations.

INTERGENERATIONAL WOUNDS: THE BAGGAGE OUR PARENTS LEFT US

Experiences of racial trauma rarely start in our lifetime, so it is helpful to look at the generations that precede us. When we explore the traumatic experiences of our parents, who were either migrants or children of migrants in a country that was overtly hostile and violent towards them because of their Blackness, we can be struck by the apparent lack of emotional response from them. They were surrounded by reminders that they did not belong. 'No Irish, no Blacks, no dogs' or 'no coloureds' comes to mind, along with similar notices placed on shop doors or property adverts that marked them, without the shadow of a doubt, as Other.

The invisibilisation of their stories of racism, bolstered by narratives of strength and resilience, masks what might be happening intergenerationally. Similarly, in the colonial context, many of us have been told about the mundane acts of humiliation and banal degradation our parents and grandparents had to endure. Stories of everyday, 'normalised' dehumanisation that came with racial oppression. Stories of being required to bow one's head before white people. Stories of being whipped within white Christian missionary schools. Stories of being spat at.

One account from my stepfather has stayed with me. It is the story of a white manager in Brazzaville disciplining a Black employee by asking him to open his mouth, spitting in the gaping orifice, then asking the Black man to swallow the phlegm. A perfect allegory, I have always thought, for colonialism. Revisiting these stories, the apparent 'lack' of emotional suffering raises alarms. Coping or defence mechanisms such as dissociating from trauma in order to survive can leave children burdened with the trauma their parents never processed.

A reminder: trauma knows no time boundary. Underestimating the consequences of trauma may result in subsequent generations being more vulnerable than their forebears. Offspring may not be aware that they are carrying and experiencing, at least in part, the trauma of their parents and forebears. A multi-level understanding of racial trauma reminds us that some of the distress we may experience is not only due to what is happening to us in the 'here and now'. It could also be caused by what happened in the 'there and then' such as the treatment of previous generations through historical atrocities, discrimination, cultural oppression and associated unprocessed wounds. Wounds that are not allowed to heal since their scab is constantly being removed within white supremacy. The past and the present shape how we experience the world and how our mental health is impacted by the world around us.

Intergenerational trauma is grossly neglected within psychological and mental health practice in the UK. This absence makes little sense. If, as we will see later in the book, silence is often a consequence of trauma, this institutional silence may well be evidence of its presence. Conceptualisations of trauma are mainly highly individualistic and centred on the psychological consequences of exposure to adverse events on single individuals. When we think about trauma at a collective level, however, we tend to think about the way entire groups of people are harmed by a single event or process or how their collective identity shifts as a result of events they may not themselves have directly experienced or witnessed[26]. It is still not exactly clear how wounds are passed on from generation to generation, but various theories exist.

For instance, Dr Harrell, whose six-part racial trauma framework we saw earlier, argues that storytelling that focuses on the hardship of those who came before us is one way to pass on trauma. So is the sharing of past survival strategies or coping mechanisms, such as being taught to put your head down and work twice as hard, being encouraged to not trust white people, and so on. Trauma may be transferred culturally by entire societies. Another African American scholar, Dr Joy DeGruy, has theorised the existence of a **Post Traumatic Slave Syndrome (PTSS)** as a form of trauma experienced by the descendants of enslaved Africans), which results from centuries of racial oppression and associated survival strategies transferred through the generations. DeGruy believes PTSS can lead to 'dysfunction' interpersonally, emotionally and behaviourally. This dysfunction may look like uncontained anger, self-neglect and difficulties with intimacy.

Unconscious communication such as psychological projection[30], which is when our thoughts, feelings and fantasies are communicated non-verbally to those around us, is also believed to be a way of passing down intergenerational trauma. Think about how terror-filled gazes from one's parents can allow for powerful messages about the world to be passed on to a child. Increasingly it is also believed that biological mechanisms (e.g. epigenetics) may be conduits to pass on such trauma[31].

Epigenetics could be described as the intersection between nature or the genes we have inherited, and nurture or life experiences or history of trauma. Adverse events and trauma can in some circumstances change the way in which DNA is expressed, and these changes can also be passed on to subsequent generations[32]. They can affect how we react to stress, adapt to various environments, our vulnerability to certain illnesses and even our mortality.

The picture of biological transmission is still unclear and disputed but researchers are trying to elucidate the mechanisms that may be involved; epigenetics is a relatively new area. Still, evidence of some transmission of harm can be found. In many cases, the children and grandchildren of trauma survivors are at increased risk of psychological distress, especially the offspring of genocidal violence[33,34]. Although most of these studies have focused on the descendants of Holocaust survivors[35], we know that in the UK, for example, children of Black migrants tend to experience more psychological distress than both their parents and their white counterparts[36]. Research has demonstrated that in the US, psychological distress appears higher too in the children of those who survived the civil rights struggle. This suggests a similar generational pattern despite the difference in circumstances. There are, of course, various factors that account for that increased level of distress within 'second and third generation' migrants and the descendants of mass trauma survivors. But the unaddressed trauma of previous generations and the conspiracies of silence around it are increasingly believed to be part of the picture.

TRAUMA AND THE BRAIN

We have known for a while that adverse experiences can fundamentally affect how our brain functions and how we experience the world. So, we can borrow from this extensive **neuroscientific** literature to understand some of the challenges some may experience as a result of racism. Dr Bessel Van der Kolk[37], a psychiatrist and world-leading expert on trauma and PTSD, argues that there are three major ways that the brain can change as a response to trauma:

1. **Our fear centre may become oversensitive.** This may translate into us becoming overwhelmed when we perceive situations as threatening. In other words, one of the oldest and most 'primitive' parts of the brain responds more easily to fear, which is why Dr Van der Kolk refers to traumatised brains as 'fear-driven brains'.

2. **Our ability to filter out what is relevant from what isn't may be compromised.** This makes it difficult to stay in the present as our attention is frequently divided and takes us either into the past or into an imagined fearful future.

3. **The part of the brain responsible for how we experience the world can change**. As a result, many trauma survivors can find it incredibly difficult to have a strong sense of who they are post-trauma.

Although these changes may not affect all of us, a closer look at neuroscience can help us better make sense of these common experiences and perhaps of some of the challenges we may experience. Four cerebral systems responsible for processing information and managing threats can change with trauma[39]:

1. **The hippocampus**
   The **hippocampus** plays a major role in learning and memory. People with histories of trauma often have abnormalities in this brain region. The hippocampus contributes to us recording new memories and retrieving them later in response to specific stimuli or events in our environment. The hippocampus also helps us distinguish between past and present. We can now better understand why feeling triggered or feeling taken back is a common experience in trauma survivors.

2. **The amygdala**
   The **amygdala's** primary role is the management of our emotional responses or emotional regulation; this includes the management of fear, anxiety and aggression. The amygdala is so implicated in the survival response

that it is sometimes thought of as a threat or danger alarm. So, the amygdala is central to how we respond to situations that remind us of, or resemble, past traumatic events. Trauma appears to increase activity in the amygdala, rendering it hypersensitive. This helps explain why trauma survivors are sensitive to distress caused by fear and anxiety and why they so often struggle with feeling safe.

3. **The prefrontal cortex**

The **prefrontal cortex** is central to the more sophisticated and complex cognitive functions such as planning, analysing or strategising, capacities sometimes referred to as the 'executive functions'. Those who have experienced significant trauma can show changes in that brain region. The prefrontal cortex is also responsible for our conscious ability to inhibit the amygdala and to manage our fears. Hence, trauma survivors often experience difficulties with thinking, memory and/or concentration; and this may be why it can be harder to manage our emotions after significant trauma.

4. **Autonomic nervous system**

The **autonomic nervous system** has been compared to a control system that regulates several bodily functions including threat-based bodily responses, such as increased heart and respiratory rate. The autonomous nervous sysytem controls our fight-or-flight and our response to stressors. When we have repeatedly been exposed to acute or chronic stress it becomes much more difficult for us to regulate our autonomic nervous system. This can explain why we may feel we have little control over our body.

HEALING TRAUMA

As we have seen, it is partly because of the changes in the brain that follow trauma that we can experience difficulties in managing fear and stress[38]. It can be why some of us may really struggle to feel safe in the world. It may be why we experience the kind of difficulties Dr Van der Kolk says are so common in trauma survivors. British clinical psychologist Professor Paul Gilbert created the **Compassion Focused Therapy** (CFT) model to redress these difficulties[39]. He also suggests that trauma and other adverse experiences such as abuse or neglect often result in individuals developing high levels of shame, self-criticalness and hostility towards them-selves. For example, by being harsh or punishing themselves when they make mistakes.

In other words, for those with a history of trauma the brain 'soothing system' or the capacity to self-reassure is not easily accessible as it is believed to be under-developed. This can cause some of us to have difficulties experiencing sanctu-ary and safeness because the neural systems that activate these feelings are thought to have been underused. Instead, self-criticalness and hostility become the way to manage emotions. This further reduces the capacity to feel safe, soothed and reassured. Further, it repeats histories of poor treatment. This is important.

The Compassion Focused Therapy framework essen-tially suggests we can increase our sense of unsafety by treating ourselves harshly. The idea is that the brain is not able to tell the difference between psychological threats (e.g. racial name calling) and physical threats (e.g. someone chas-ing us with a knife). Crucially, our brain also cannot tell the difference between external threats (what comes from the social world (e.g. racial discrimination) and what comes from within (e.g. self-hate). Our brain responds the same way in all cases, triggering fear in our threat centre, and our fight-or-flight response via complex hormonal and neurobiological events. The impact of trauma on the brain does not have to be a life sentence. Our brains are not immutable and continue to grow and change throughout life. Reparative experiences, and relevant mindful deliberate action following trauma, can fundamentally alter our brain structure too. The idea that experiences can shape our cerebral environment and brain structures is referred to as **neuroplasticity**[38]. And so, we can heal from trauma. In the context of white supremacy healing must be deliberate, targeted and a lifelong journey. Our first task is to do what we can to counteract external and internal threats.

Encouragingly, there are steps we can take to help ensure we do not unnecessarily create unsafeness for ourselves[40]; and we can learn to practise self-soothing and relaxation to counteract that which racism may have caused. In the following chapters these strategies will be explored.

— SUMMARY —

1.

Black people continue to be poorly served within white institutions. In this chapter we considered race inequalities within the mental health system and their consequences for Black people.

2.

Racial trauma, which as a framework aims to make visible the harm of racism, must be considered beyond the individual. The intergenerational transmission of trauma that may take place via various mechanisms likely contributes to the excess of psychological distress in Black groups.

3.

Our brain can change as a result of trauma and adverse experiences. Such changes can result in us having difficulties feeling soothed and safe, and in us becoming prone to shame, which in turn can compromise our sense of safety in the world.

4.

Adverse experiences and trauma can fundamentally alter how we process information, relate to the world, and relate to ourselves. It is thus important we understand the basic neurobiology of trauma, so we may understand why our bodies and minds respond in the way they do and understand what may help reverse the damage of racism.

In the next chapter, **BLACK SHAME**, we consider the specific ways in which racism can enter our minds and harm our mental health by examining the psychological world of Blackness.

RACE REFLECTIONS

You have explored the institutional context of Black mental health and the impact of the past on our contemporary experiences of racism. This section gives you the opportunity to reflect and develop skills to help resist and help protect your mental health from racism.

What did you find most challenging in this chapter?

You may want to explore the physical responses, images and thoughts that came to you and explore what they might take you back to. Please use the Race Reflections reflective model (p.207) to help you.

....

....

....

....

....

It is impossible to understand Black mental health without understanding the impact of historical trauma.

When it comes to your history, what event(s) have shaped your experience of the world?

....

....

....

....

....

Current definitions of mental health problems may not necessarily reflect the challenges we face in the world. Still, it is important to think about what keeps us well and actively seek to stay well.

What is mental health to you/what does being well look like to you? Think about ways you can incorporate social justice and community building in your definition.

....

....

....

....

....

For various reasons seeking help can be difficult for many of us. Accepting that we, like anyone else, are deserving of support and care humanises us, as does connecting with the community around us. Tapping into community and social support also acts as a protective factor.

Who forms your support network? Who can you call on if distressed? What may you need to do to sustain and nurture relationships with people in your network?

....

....

....

....

....

ACTION POINT
PRACTISE GRATITUDE

Trauma makes us sensitive to possible threats in our environment. This focus on or disposition to notice things that are threatening and painful can contribute to emotional distress and keep our internal world out of balance. We need to be conscious and deliberate in paying attention to the little things that make life worth living, the things we are grateful for amid the injustice. Furthermore, practising gratitude is linked to better wellbeing[35].

Your action point is: Commit to recording in your journal at least one thing (and up to three) for which you are grateful, every day.

It could be something as simple as the sun on your skin on a particularly glorious day, an act of kindness towards you, the smile or comfort a friend or child gave to you, a good laugh, or a good read. Practising gratitude is a helpful way to rebalance our attention and connect differently to the world.

CHAPTER 3

BLACK SHAME

What does it really feel like to live in a society that repeatedly tells you that you are not welcome and, that you do not belong? This chapter explores these questions.

Extraordinarily little has been written about the lived experience and psychological impact of racism. In this chapter we delve into the ways in which racism enters our mind and body and wreaks havoc with our internal worlds, generation after generation. We also look at why so many of us are likely to, at some point in our life, experience psychological distress. To do this we will consider shame, injustice and homelessness as central elements in Black people's experiences of the world and examine their impact on our psychological functioning.

INTERSECTIONALITY AND TRAUMA

Case study: Fiona

Fiona, a 55-year-old woman of mixed heritage, has seen both her parents being racially abused. In particular, as a young child she witnessed her Black father being chased by a racist mob. Fiona's mother, a white migrant, could not cope with the racism. The family unit disintegrated. Fiona was taken into care. In care, Fiona's cultural needs as a mixed-race child were erased. She was regularly racially harassed, to the point she attempted to rub the Blackness out of her skin with scrubbing pads and bleach. Fiona reported experiencing racism often at the hands of the police.

She was also sexually abused in care and when she tried to speak of her abuse to social services she was not believed. Fiona also shared some of her experiences as an adult. Once, when she confronted a neighbour who had racially harassed her, the police were called and went on to arrest Fiona. The racial components of the dispute and its response were ignored. Fiona's complaints were dismissed. Fiona described an incident she faced, much later in life, during her studies: Within a child observation class, a 'mixed-race' child was described as 'Mediterranean' by a fellow (white) student. Her attempts at exploring what she considered to be an act of 'subtle middle-class racism' were ignored. Fiona described how for a year after this event, she went on to have nightmares in which she was beating up the student who had erased the Blackness of the child.

Fiona's trauma is complex and centred around racism. Racism was the main cause for the distress her mother experienced, the catalyst for the family separation, the reason for the self-hatred Fiona experienced, and the source of her having her cultural identity erased. In addition to racial abuse, Fiona suffered sexual abuse, which is also instrumental to her vulnerability and trauma history. Acts of racial injustice may have amplified or triggered memories of interpersonal trauma such as Fiona's sexual abuse, leading to the reproduction of messages of inferiority.

Fiona's unexpressed rage at her violent gendered and racialised objectification manifested in those nightmares. One may argue this is an act of displacement of the repressed anger she may feel towards whiteness and/or her white mother, both of which may have come to symbolise abandonment, dismissal and erasure. There are parallels between her initial experience of being silenced about her sexual abuse and the way her experience of racism has been consistently denied within various social structures such as the police and mental health services. Fiona spoke to me about her body and her belief that racism contributed to her getting breast cancer. (In Chapter 4, we will look at the impact of racism on the body.)

UNDERSTANDING INTERSECTIONALITY

Experiences of racial injustice and racism are inextricably linked to other, non-race-related experiences of injustice, trauma and other axes of oppression. African American law Professor and feminist Kimberlé Crenshaw[1] coined the term **intersectionality** to conceptualise how combined systems of oppression (e.g. gender, race, sexuality, class, age, religion and disability) are interconnected. They lead to varying experiences and vulnerability to subordination and discrimination. Research on this is starting to emerge. Large-scale statistical analyses have shown that the number of marginalised groups and the frequency of discrimination have more explanatory power when it comes to measuring risk of developing PTSD than when considering contextual factors alone. Those who have experienced more adversities in life tend to be more distressed when faced with racism and racial injustice. Therefore, intersectional lenses are required to make sense of Black people's experiences and the nuances of anti-Blackness.

More widely, people affected by racial trauma often have non-racism-related trauma histories. I have worked with individuals who after being exposed to racism-related abuses started to have flashbacks of childhood experiences of sexual abuse. In my own research, participants who had experienced more interpersonal trauma, such as being separated from parents as children and/or being bullied, appeared to experience more distress when faced with racial injustice. I have thus argued that racial trauma intersects with other experiences of injustice and trauma. Research on gendered racism has found that multiple oppressions are generally associated with increased psychological distress[2].

MORE ON SHAME

As we have seen in Chapter 2, all trauma survivors must contend with shame.

When it comes to Blackness, from the treatment of our ancestors to enduring race inequalities and racial hostility, we are deeply affected and shaped by racial injustice and what happened in the past and this includes the violence and shame our forebears experienced. Shame results in low self-worth, identification with those who harm us, silence and suppressed feelings. Shame or malignant shame is equally transmissible. Oppressed groups, including Black people, are governed by shame and in turn we learn to navigate the world through shame. The cycles of shame-based abuse and self-relating or policing are transmitted on.

Shame exists at various levels. The late French West Indian psychiatrist and postcolonial author, Frantz Fanon[3], in *Black Skin, White Masks*, eloquently described how colonialism has distorted Black people's understanding of their Blackness, as we come to internalise white colonisers' gaze and racist constructions of savagery, inferiority and deficiency. These constructions continue to lead to deep feelings of shame and self-hatred, which many of us attempt to reconcile by rejecting aspects of our Blackness. The politics of **assimilation** and of **respectability** speak of this shame. They are therefore based on self-hate. Although they may provide temporary escape and possibly material gain and conditional access to structures of power, they reproduce white supremacy and as such breed further shame and self-alienation. Self-contempt, disdain and scorn were not merely accidental by-products of colonialism – they were manufactured, deliberate colonial weapons to fortify whiteness and reduce resistance. But the toxic shame we are talking about is not only a colonial residue nor is it only related to race and racism.

When we are harmed systematically and repeatedly, eventually we start to believe that we deserve that which is done to us. It follows in our thinking that there is something deeply broken and dysfunctional about us. Trauma survivors often adopt these beliefs. **Patriarchy** offers an alternative and intersecting system of subjugation upon which this reality can be observed, often across a range of traumas. For instance, physically and sexually abused women tend to feel a deep sense of shame over their abuse. Male, cisgendered perpetrators of gendered violence clearly have stakes in women or in their victims experiencing shame. Not least because it reduces the possibility of accountability; in fact, it shifts it altogether by silently encouraging women to self-blame and self-hate for the sexual violence they have experienced, rendering them much less likely to speak out and seek justice.

Similarly, the myth of meritocracy is reproduced when poor and socially disadvantaged groups feel shame for not achieving the social 'success' of their more privileged counterparts[4]. When inadequacy rather than unjust disadvantage is internalised as an explanatory model, it is less likely that unfair structures will be dismantled. Shame takes hold and devours the will to resist and dissent. The impact of racism on Black bodies and minds is partly mediated by introjected shame so that each spit, insult, microaggression and act of exclusion reminds us that we are Other. That somehow, we are responsible. We are to blame. This leads naturally to intensified and chronic distress. A distress that is often unaddressed because it is also subject to shame.

Since we are supposed to be both inhuman and superhuman, or inhuman because we are superhuman[5], when these internalised notions of Black strength, resilience and invulnerability do not match our lived reality we may feel inadequate. This further increases our distress and provides additional evidence that we are not enough. As there is also shame and stigma around mental health difficulties in our communities, some of this stigma is independent from the mental health inequalities encountered in Chapter 1; we are much less likely to seek help and instead may opt to suffer in silence and in shame. That shame and stigma cannot be separated from long-standing association between Blackness and madness, Blackness and psychological or intellectual inferiority and related cultural inheritances.

Shame is not only used by abusers to manipulate our emotions. Often, it also functions as a compass to evaluate our worth, or as evidence of our lack of the same. As a result, when we experience shame, we may become fearful that speaking of it may lead others to evaluate us in the way we evaluate ourselves. To know we are worthless rather than to know that we feel worthless. Basically, to be found out. Perhaps this helps explain why shame can be difficult to 'own up' and speak about[6].

THE IMPACT OF INJUSTICE

As Black people, there is no single part of our existence that has not been touched by injustice – directly or indirectly. I do not consider the events laid out in this book to be unusual. Nor do I consider myself or the people who come to see me for support to be outliers when it comes to our experience of racism. As mentioned in Chapter 1, there is something dysfunctional in how we define psychological dysfunction or in how we define mental health problems[7]. I tend to think of mental health problems as acts of resistance to injustice that sometimes have undesired or unintended effects. The erasure of the impact of injustice within mental health frameworks is another failing that serves whiteness. There is nothing pathological in being hurt, affected and destabilised by injustice in the world. It is what makes us human. There is no glory in adapting to injustice and inhumanity, contrary to what mental health practices often tell us. Each time we socialise ourselves into accepting injustice we cut ourselves off from parts of our humanity. We normalise social inequality and add a layer of protection to an already solid status quo.

The lived experience of injustice is central to the excess of psychological distress we experience. I have long proposed that it leads to a form of '**ontological insecurity**': chronic feelings of unsafeness and detachment in the world. When we face injustice and we recognise it as such, our self-image often shifts. Our relationships with the world and with ourselves are often affected[8]. Our sense of belonging and being in the world can become shaky. Our world is transformed. I believe the need for justice is anchored deeply within us. Through our lived experience of racial injustice, social inequalities become internal events, they take hold and lodge themselves within our body. It is not coincidental that the experiences that most accurately predict psychological distress, such as bullying, discrimination, sexual abuse, poverty and even bereavement, seem to all involve a breached sense of justice. This breach of the principle or expectation of justice seems to profoundly distress us.

Reflecting upon my own clinical work, I do not believe that I have ever met a single person in distress who was not struggling with injustice one way or the other. From the persecuted asylum seeker who feels God's fury has turned on them despite devoting their entire life to religion. To the child who cannot comprehend why they are the one being picked on at school for being 'different'. From the parents struggling to say goodbye to a dying child. To those who have been laid off because of ageism or sexism. To those whose body was objectified in the most degrading ways. Injustice turns us into robots. Injustice despairs us. Injustice wounds us deeply. No amount of psychological support can ever help an entire group thrive without addressing unjust social structures and racial injustice[9].

WHAT WE CALL 'HOME'

Case study: Eileen

Eileen (pronouns: they/she) is a non-binary Black patient I spoke to as part of my research. Eileen was admitted to hospital in London with suspected multiple sclerosis. Once there they quickly noticed they were treated differently from white patients. They told me that during the rounds when they got to their bed, the way in which staff would address them was completely different to everyone else. Other patients might get a 'good morning' while they would get a 'so we are looking at your file' and there wouldn't even be a greeting. When they were acknowledged, their body was handled with contempt or hostility. They felt man-handled and as though there were little regard for the discomfort they were caused. Convinced these experiences in the hospital ward were due to their Blackness, they made complaints, which were dismissed. They returned home. Their health deteriorated. They started to urinate blood and then became blind in one eye. They did not seek support for several weeks, remaining in pain and at home. When I asked them why they had not sought help, they said they could no longer be sure they could trust their body, due to being told so many times that they were wrong in their experience. The impact of repeated experience of denial had altered Eileen's relationship with their body and with reality. How many of us have come to doubt our own reality when it is denied in situations of racism?

DENIAL, SHAME AND INJUSTICE

The denial of racism can have serious consequences. Denial is part of the cycle of abuse. Some researchers have conceptualised it as secondary injury akin to 'rubbing toxins into an open wound'. Silencing or denial significantly increase distress after initial racist incidents. Yet covert or subtle racism makes it virtually impossible to objectively establish the occurrence or non-occurrence of racism beyond the **embodied** experiences of the person at the receiving end of it, lending itself particularly well to that process of internal displacement. An uprooting of marginalised people from their internal home due to chronic **gaslighting** when they attempt to speak of their experience of the world is enacted through the misuse of power. Is it any wonder that so many Black people are vulnerable to diagnoses of psychosis or become dissociated from their own reality like Eileen, when the home that is their sense of truth and reality is chronically rendered precarious? This is what I have previously referred to as '**epistemic homelessness**'. I argue that our capacity to know is dependent on our capacity to have a home.

In 2017, in preparation for my TEDx Talk on the subject, I ran a few polls on social media. I asked three questions[8,9]:

Firstly, whether people of colour found covert or overt racism more challenging. Five hundred and forty-nine people answered. Covert racism was found to be about seven times more challenging. Second, I asked about the outcome of conversations about subtle discrimination. The results were that a whopping 95% said they were mocked, ignored, or not believed when they named their experience of subtle racism. Finally, I enquired about the impact of such invalidation. The most common feeling reported was that one was 'losing one's mind', which was experienced by 36% of participants, followed by 32% saying that they felt pain or were in distress. Other reported feelings included rage, helplessness, exhaustion, shame, disbelief and being gaslighted.

These findings are consistent with my own clinical experience and with other research findings on the serious psychological impact of **microaggressions**. The term racial microaggressions was coined by African American psychiatrist Dr Chester Pierce to describe everyday and often subtle insults, indignities and dismissals experienced by Americans of colour and which affected their mental health[10]. Experiences of covert bigotry often create much more race-based distress than more overt and direct expressions of racism. Not only are the triggering effects of strategically ambiguous words or deeds often loaded with racial denigration, Black targets are often left to do hours of cognitive work. Hours of hypothesis testing. Hours of rumination. Hours replaying, often second by second, what was said or what was done, in the hope of trusting that they know what they do indeed know. Gaslighting ourselves and in doing so, reproducing the contempt this society holds toward our capacity to know, and our authority.

SHAKY HOMES, SHAKY ATTACHMENTS

We traditionally speak of attachment to focus on the infant – caregiver bond[11] and its long-lasting impact on how we come to experience relationships and the world[12]. Outside of mental health disciplines, others have interrogated the importance of place in terms of human functioning and orientation. Increasingly, there is scrutiny over the emotional bonds or attachments that exist between locations and people.

Place attachment refers to the strong emotional bond we develop with a specific location[13]. Like infant and caregiver attachments, our relationship with places is reciprocal, and shaped by how we are responded to as well as by the nature of our experiences. Place attachment is thought to be composed of two intersecting dimensions: a sense of rootedness and of sense of place. Rootedness is related to history, ancestry and lineage. It is the sense of familiarity that arises with habitual residence over time. Sense of place, on the other hand, is more subjective. It is to do with meaning–making, the symbolic connection and internal narratives we hold about locations. Place attachment helps us to think and make sense of our relationship with the world.

Homeness, homelessness and belonging are central themes in Black groups' experiences of psychological distress[14]. Through our history of displacement and immigration, homelessness has huge significance. As a result of the transatlantic slave trade, many of us have been born away from our ultimate ancestral lands. This disconnection already renders home-making complex. In addition, our sense of homeness is rendered precarious by immigration and associated racism and xenophobia. It is tough to feel secure in one's home when your skin forever marks you as an outsider. As not belonging. As not really from 'here', especially when the threat of dispossession or deportation always looms. Racism compromises cultural affiliation and the sense of home. How can your home be truly your home if entry into it and your right of abode is conditional? When this right can so easily be denied under the racist fantasy that some other home will always be yours for you to claim and return to. Even when that connection barely exists. Even if that presumed home is in fact much more unfamiliar than your usual place of dwelling[15].

WINDRUSH AND THE HOSTILE
ENVIRONMENT

The hostile environment[16] refers to successive sets of policies and legislative measures implemented by the Home Office specifically designed to render the United Kingdom hostile and inhospitable for those migrants it deemed to have no legal right to remain in the UK. The bulk of the hostile environment measures came into action with the Immigration Act 2014 and have since been expanded under subsequent legislations. In everyday terms, the hostile environment meant the state making it as hard as possible for migrants to work, to find housing, to access healthcare, to open bank accounts. And of course, since whiteness belongs and blackness does not, naturally, those with Black skin, the forever aliens of the land, were disproportionately impacted. The Windrush atrocity provides an illustration of the racialisation of 'home'.

The term 'Windrush Generation' refers to those people from the Caribbean who came to the UK between 1948 and 1973, invited to fill Britain's post-war labour shortage and help rebuild the nation. The name 'Windrush' originates from the HMT *Empire Windrush* ship, which carried one of the largest and earliest groups in 1948. Because the Caribbean was, at the time, a part of the British Commonwealth, those who arrived were automatically British subjects and free to permanently live and work in the UK. Still, these citizens were required to 'prove' decades later their right to live in the UK through draconian and inhuman processes that resulted in hundreds unable to document their status. In addition, the Home Office have reportedly destroyed the records of many.

As a result, families were broken, parents, children, siblings separated, loving partners torn apart, multi-generations of relatives traumatised by a British immigration system appearing to be set on inflicting violence on those whose bodies it deemed no longer of value. Bodies who had a right to be in the UK all along. Bodies that were deemed expendable and could therefore be subjected to bureaucratic degradation and routine humiliation. It left many ill, suicidal and distraught. At least 11 of the wrongly deported have died. Numbers are disputed. Disputed but, of course, not tracked.

At the time of writing and despite the government issuing an apology[17], most survivors are still to receive the support and compensation promised to them. It is hard to miss that those displaced from their land and shipped to the other end of the world were once more being treated like disposable cargo shippable to 'the Americas'. The trauma of such border violence combined with a history of separation and displacement is severe. Although it hit right in the heart of people of Caribbean heritage, subsequent waves of people from the Commonwealth at large have also been affected by the hostile environment and faced degradation, deportation and violence.

With immigration comes dislocation. Individuals and groups are extracted from their homes and from what they know. This displacement shifts how we experience ourselves and our identity. It disrupts the sense of the familiar. Contact with roots and cultural bearings lose their proximity. Family and friends often fade into memories. Often bloodied memories. This sense of loss and disconnection can be profound and can last for generations. Affecting those displaced. Their children. And those who come after. It is no coincidence that displacement is associated with psychological distress and poor mental health[18]. Feeling disconnected causes psychological distress. Psychological distress in turn causes further disconnection.

A framework that has been developed to describe the ongoing struggle to find a home among those whose identities sit at the crossroad of two cultures or more, is that of **cultural homelessness**[19]. We are said to feel culturally homeless when we are neither quite at home within the cultures of our parents or heritage nor that of the country we were born or reside in. Often, due to repeated experience of marginalisation, discrimination, or exclusion in both or all cultures. It is the sense of not feeling quite at home anywhere. Cultural homelessness can leave us feeling vulnerable, unprotected, and forever in search of a sense of belonging. This cultural alienation and yearning are part of the puzzle of mental health inequalities.

Finally, there is another level of homelessness that we barely speak about honestly, related to the alleged story of Black betrayal. The ultimate 'Black on Black violence', some say. It is unspoken mainly because of the trauma and shame around it. This is one of the most painful Black conversations. Growing up, it was a constant presence in my relationship with people of Caribbean heritage. It carried centuries of pain and unaddressed wounds that exist across the diaspora.

These notions are rooted in anti-Blackness. No one says of WWI or WWII that they started because white people started to kill other white people, or takes them as illustrations of 'white on white violence'. It is a reality that conflicts tend to occur between those who are in proximity. And, throughout history there have always been collaborators in situations of war, conflict and oppression. Black history and the history of the transatlantic slave trade is no different. It is absolutely without a shadow of a doubt that there were African collaborators who out of fear, coercion or for material gain supported the slave trade. Slave catchers who were Africans, kings who sold prisoners from enemy tribes to Europeans. But there were also millions of people resisting and fighting slavers. This history has not reached the stories we tell ourselves and this is not a coincidence. The systematic destruction of colonial and imperial documents and the re-telling of our history through the white gaze and its associated 'recollections' and distortions has resulted in the widespread erasure of this reality. Carrying the belief consciously or otherwise that your ancestors were sold while there was no attempt to resist, to stop them from leaving the shores of Africa, that even your ancestors sought to get rid of you, leaves you vulnerable to feeling unwanted. The sense of homelessness is reproduced at ancestral levels. We must therefore add nuance to this story and remember the impact of such historical lies and half-truths.

─── SUMMARY ───

1.

Experiences of shame, injustice and homelessness are central to the psychological distress of Black people. These considerations are often absent from conversations on mental health.

2.

When considering responses to racism it is vital that we consider other experiences of trauma, adverse life experiences, as well as other axes of oppression. This is what I refer to as the intersection of trauma.

3.

Injustices may leave an imprint on the soul, which fundamentally shifts our relationship with our self, our body and the world. But every system is reliant on those it harms believing they deserve the harm and violence aimed at them.

4.

Externalising this belief alone would do so much for our collective mental health. Externalising this belief is therefore a matter of public health.

The next chapter, **BLACK BODIES**, discusses the physical consequences of racism and explores the physical demands and violence carried out on Black people.

RACE REFLECTIONS

Shame, injustice and homelessness are specific ways we may come to be harmed by racism – this section gives you the opportunity to reflect and develop skills to resist and protect your mind from racism.

What was the most challenging aspect of this chapter for you?

You may want to explore your physical responses, images and thoughts that came to you and explore what they might take you back to. Please use the Race Reflections reflective model (p.207) to help you.

....

....

....

....

....

Shame is a powerful emotion that often accompanies trauma.

You are invited to reflect on your experiences of shame. What brings on feelings of shame in you? What do you tend to do when you feel ashamed? Where might you have learnt to respond in this way and what are the pros and cons?

....

....

....

....

....

We have learnt the centrality of injustice in our experience of the world.

What is your relationship to injustice? How do you tend to respond when you witness injustice or are treated unjustly? How do your reactions relate to your previous experience of injustice? What helps you get a sense of justice?

....

....

....

....

....

We are often shaped by our caregivers/our parents' experiences of the world even when these experiences appear not to have affected them.

What significant life events have your parents experienced that might have shaped their worldview and the messages they have communicated to you about the world?

....

....

....

....

....

ACTION POINT
STRENGTHEN HOMENESS

Your action point: Before you complete *Living While Black* you are invited to increase your sense of homeness. Think about your home in as many contexts as you can such as your physical home, your cultural home, your '**epistemic**' home and take steps to make each of these homes as comfortable and safe as you can.

In terms of your physical home, can you think of ways to make it feel more welcoming and safe to you? If you don't have an entire house, can you make your room as comfortable as possible? What could you do to want to spend more time in this space? To make it feel more secure and homely? In terms of your cultural home, how many cultural homes do you have? Some actions can increase our sense of connection to a culture, such as learning and speaking the language, and regularly visiting and/or learning about the place's history.

For your 'epistemic' home, learn to trust your experience and your body. Your beliefs, the ways your body lets you know what is real or what is not. Your body and mind primarily exist to keep you safe. How might you remind yourself of this?

CHAPTER 4

BLACK BODIES

You get into a room. It is a white space.

As you enter, you feel a sense of heaviness. You look around and notice pairs of eyes staring as though devouring you. You instantly realise you are the only person of colour in the space. A sort of malaise takes hold of you. You feel a little queasy. Perhaps the discomfort starts to make you feel dizzy. You may experience nausea. You might attempt to stick around and impose your presence, in silence. You may even take a seat but in any case, your body is reacting to something. Soon enough that something becomes overwhelming. Every move you make is with microscopic precision as self-consciousness takes over your body. Your Blackness is in sharp closeup from the outside in. You know you want to exit now. You know this space is inhospitable to you. It may start to feel hard to breathe and so you try to look for a way out and a reason to leave, discreetly. You find one and you disappear almost as quickly as you entered. Your departure likely goes unnoticed. What happened in that room? What was your body reacting to? Is this only anxiety or have you been expelled from that space? Whose fantasy were you acting out?[1]

This chapter centres on the Black body. The Black body as a site of violence, but also the Black body as site of contestation. The impact of racism often finds itself lodged in the Black body. So, in this chapter, in order to further our understanding of racial trauma on Black groups, we examine how Black bodies become permeated by whiteness. How they are transformed and shaped by white supremacy and the impact of racist violence, how even when psychological, affects our physical health.

The above scenario illustrates how quickly and covertly we can be policed and consumed. How powerfully and yet invisibly we can be excluded. It is a painful reminder that in the white imagination there are still so few spaces we can rightfully claim as ours. Furthermore, I have no doubt that to most Black readers, walking into a hostile white space will be known if not cognitively then through their body. Most of us have been taught to discount knowledge that we acquire through our body, our embodied experience of the world. Partly this is due to whiteness and its hyper-rational aspirations. Partly this is because as Black people we have been taught to replace our subjectivity or our experience of the world with that of those who do us harm. Partly this is a survival strategy, and intergenerational trauma too. So, we learn to be suspicious of our senses ourselves and ignore what our body tells us about that world, in the same way as, again, ancestral and indigenous traditions were erased through colonialism.

BLACK BODIES, WHITE FANTASIES

We started this chapter by using an expression many will find controversial. Many may feel that using the term 'Black bodies' is dehumanising. The use of 'body' rather than person is multi-fold. Firstly, it emphasises the fact that we are racialised as Black because of the characteristics of our body. Second, the expression stresses that the violence done to us is often done onto our bodies. Our bodies therefore are sites of racial violence, not necessarily our personhood.

There is a long history of emphasising the politics of the body within social justice and critical scholarship for through colonialism very reasons. But also, to challenge Cartesian thought, which splits bodily experiences from the intellectual domain, I also seek to honour the knowledge we gather from our body or what I refer to as 'embodied data'. Finally, and this is a point that American Jamaican poet and playwright Claudia Rankine makes: our bodies arouse fantasies in the white mind, which rob us of our personhood. It is the image of Blackness that is seen and that image of Blackness is not that of a sibling, it is not that of a son or child, or of a friend. It is a Black body that needs restraining, containing or neutralising.

> 'When white men are shooting Black people, some of it is malice and some an out-of-control image of Blackness in their minds. Darren Wilson told the jury that he shot Michael Brown because he looked like a demon. And I do not disbelieve it. Blackness in the white imagination has nothing to do with Black people.'[2]
>
> Guardian interview with Claudia Rankine

This quote makes a partial reference to the grotesque killing of Michael Brown that took place on 9 August 2014 in Ferguson. Michael Brown was just 18 when he was killed by officer Darren Wilson, who was 28. The story starts with Brown and his friend Dorian Johnson leaving a convenience store and ends with him being shot 12 times. The final shot was in the head. Facts remain contested and of course Brown took his side of the story to the grave. At the crime scene, Brown's body was left to lie on the streets for four and a half hours. In court, Wilson describes Brown as though he were a monster, an out-of-control wild animal full of rage, aggressive, hostile, 'crazy' and threatening his life. He described him as a 'demon' making a 'grunting . . . aggravated sound'[3]. Wilson was found not guilty, and the rest is now history.

THE WHITE GAZE

Black Skin, White Masks[4] was the first book to examine the psychology of racism and the internalisation of whiteness. It also revealed the impact of white **projections** on the Black body.

Racial hatred has long been thought of as a form of protection against these aspects of the self, others or the world that white people find intolerable. Projection is a **defence mechanism** that occurs when usually unpalatable parts of the self are disowned and attributed to others[5]. Projection may be used to defend against one's sexual urges. To defend against one's immorality or sense of depravity. Or to defend against the fear of the unknown. More broadly speaking, to protect oneself against uncertainty, powerlessness and the fear of death, some of the most primal anxieties.

Projection is therefore a way of cleansing the self by ridding it of those aspects that clash with its sense of goodness. Let's translate this into racial dynamics. In a society where the often overvalued so-called rationality is used as the only or superior way to know and access truth, the emotional and more embodied self will naturally be difficult to tolerate. The Black body will therefore serve as a convenient repository of irrationality and bodily impulses. Similarly, if aggression and sexual impulses clash with white puritan or Christian constructions of innocence, chastity and bodily mastery then, of course, the Black body will become the carrier of sexual depravity, aggression and impulsivity in the white imagination.

COLONIALISM: THE ONGOING WEIGHT OF THE PAST

Our starting point to contextualise the treatment of the Black body is Western colonialism. Today it informs our Othering in white spaces, an experience that arguably unites all Black bodies on earth. As a political and socio-economic endeavour, colonialism encompassed the exploitation and control of large areas of the world. With that came replacing colonised countries' political sovereignty with some foreign metropolitan authority or administration. Colonialism involved taking over natural resources, lands and bodies deemed commodities. It compromised both the colonised and the coloniser's humanity.

The former ceased to exist as persons as they were stripped of everything that made them human and the latter embodied atrocious violence and the power to possess, dispossess and exercise brutal control. By acquiring partial or complete control over foreign regions and/or by occupying them with settlers, colonialism was the ultimate intrusive violence, the ultimate breach of boundaries. It was rape in every sense of the word. And, the boundaries breached went well beyond the geographical.

One of the ways colonialism came to be self-sustained was through the mind of the colonised. The colonising of minds was carried out primarily by imposing racialised hierarchies topped by whiteness. This transformed the colonised sense of self and the world and led to the internalisation of racist myths and constructions such as the inferiority of Black and brown people. The psychological warfare waged by colonialism on Black minds also included the erasure of indigenous cultures and belief systems, which created both internal and external disturbances. The long-term impact of colonialism continues to attract much attention and controversy. Although there is really nothing controversial in stating that long-lasting systems of organising every aspect of the world including power relations would in some way leave some residues behind. Most of the past 500 years have been spent convinced of the intellectual inferiority of Black people, policing the Black body, ascribing it to designated territories and subservient roles and ensuring it did not move beyond its station. Where did all this stuff go?

There are various ways to think about the ongoing impact of the machinery of modern colonialism and how it continues to shape our existence. Post-colonialism, neo-colonialism and coloniality offer a few helpful frameworks. **Post-colonialism** is first and foremost the academic study of the legacy of colonialism and imperialism. **Neo-colonialism,** a branch of post-colonial interest, deals with the way new forms of domination and subordination arose after colonised nations became 'independent'. It focuses on the contemporary strategies former colonial powers use to keep exploiting these countries by making them dependent, subjugated and indebted. Finally, coloniality refers to the long-standing patterns of relations that emerged because of **colonialism**, which continue to define our culture, power relations, intersubjective exchanges and knowledge production. Each of these areas attract their fair bit of criticism, much of it defensive and misconceived and beyond the scope of the current chapter.

One enduring line of criticism is linguistic. Some people have argued that the prefixes 'neo' and 'post'[6] create the illusion of discontinuity and ending. We could argue this puts an arbitrary boundary between the present and the past. There is indeed a tendency to distance ourselves from the unpalatable by relaying it to that mythical space we call 'the past'. A form of dissociation that helps 'us' avoid revisiting colonial atrocities and contemporary complicity. Still, relations of domination and subjugation manifest in various spaces and need to be contextualised. In many ways, as many have suggested, they are neither 'accidental' nor 'incidental'; rather they reflect the continuation of colonialism. And the reproduction of the past into the present[7].

THE BLACK BODY AND BOUNDARIES

There are various ways to understand psychological or psychic boundaries. Fundamentally, holding boundaries means separating psychological entities. It means separating our emotions, thoughts and beliefs or our internal world from that of others. It can be argued that boundaries form lines that stop us from merging into others and stop others from merging into us. They consequently keep the integrity of our personhood intact. That ability to preserve our personal integrity (boundaries) has been called personal sovereignty[7] and concerns our capacity to protect our psychological independence, self-governance, self-determination and freedom from unwanted authority, interference or intrusion.

It governs how we move, how much or how little space we take up, the distance or proximity between us, the relationship between our bodies and places – all this tells us something about our socio-political and historical contexts. There are various ways to assert and communicate dominance and superiority. And the ways in which bodies move through space and are treated in space are good indicators of power relations. The interconnection between body, space and historical racism will therefore become manifest and experienced through bodies. From the spreading of legs, to subtly elbowing us out of proximity, to the disregarding of physical boundaries and the invisibilisation of our bodies. The expectation that the Black body gives way to the white body. I remember how once, on a busy London bus full of white bodies with no seat available, an older white woman got on and went straight to a Black woman to ask for her to get up. The Black body she displaced was disabled. This only became apparent when she got up and struggled to stand with a walking stick. A Black woman was asked to make space for a white woman amid the sea of white bodies. She was the body that was required to be displaced. This entitlement to space also reflects the entitlement to Black bodies, particularly to Black women's bodies[8].

Case study: Julie

A study group is joined by one person of colour, the only one. She is Black and initially welcomed by the group, who says it is keen to have someone of a 'different' background. Julie, the newest group member, quickly notices microaggressions and other forms of exclusionary behaviour that contradict verbalised discourses of inclusion the group holds dear. She raises the matter and attempts to get her peers to understand the impact of their behaviour on her. Although she appears to be listened to, there is no verbal engagement with her experience. The covert behaviours remain and raising the matter results in her being ignored and eventually marginalised. Julie becomes overtly distressed, angry and emotionally uncontained and is eventually excluded from the group.

Beverley Stobo[9], one of very few Black group analysts (a specialist in group dynamics/processes), suggests the silence that occurs when racism is raised serve to regulate and manage the anxiety it produces. This silence holds a contentious space in between white groups and Black people, according to Stobo. A space that holds the fear and terror of something that is too difficult, if not impossible, to name: shared trauma-laden histories of **imperialism**, colonialism and enslavement. What is feared and too painful to put into words is a discovery or acknowledgement of racism.

We can use this formulation to understand Julie's experience and the group's responses to her. Julie was initially welcomed into the group, who no doubt saw itself as liberal and possibly above racism. Unsurprisingly, as Julie tried to articulate the racism, which was becoming apparent and targeted at her, these dynamics could not be contained. The group was conflicted about its racism and could neither express it directly nor confront it when invited to. As Julie attempted to make conscious the racism by directly confronting it, the difficulty in communication – the group disturbance – was located in her. She was selected to carry the burden of it, alone. Containing the disturbance led to her becoming uncontained. She became distressed while white group members could through their lack of emotional display maintain a facade of 'objectivity', emotional maturity, detachment and separation from the disturbance or problem they had co-created in the first place, and which belonged to them. Succeeding in excluding Julie and therefore in splitting off from their racism.

SCAPEGOATS: THE CONSEQUENCE OF NAMING THE PROBLEM

British-Australian feminist Professor Sara Ahmed teaches us that when we speak of a problem, we become the problem[10]. In other words, speakers of problems become problems who speak. In every case of scapegoating, there is displacement and misdirection. Often uncomfortable or unacceptable feelings such as anger, envy and shame are displaced and redirected onto another member, a colleague, a peer often, but not always a more vulnerable person or group. The scapegoat can then be persecuted, bullied or treated unfairly as those who project onto them are able to discharge their own (uncontained and un-metabolised) stuff[11,12].

Some of the conditions associated with scapegoating include:

1) **A blame culture** where there is a need to quickly find someone to blame when things go wrong or not according to plan;

2) **Highly hierarchical cultures** where power is unequally distributed, and decision-making is more vertical than horizontal;

3) **Distressed contexts** when individuals might be experiencing high levels of stress and anxiety perhaps because of organisational restructuring, change or any increased sense of insecurity;

4) **Contexts of underrepresentation** where some groups or individuals may be demographically isolated or 'the only one'.

INTERNALISING PROJECTIONS

When we think about projections as a defence mechanism it is important to remember that they may or may not stick to the recipient. In psychology we call the process of making projections stick **projective identification**. With projective identification the material, feelings, impulses, thoughts or fantasies stick because they are forced onto the recipient to make them feel or behave in a way that is consistent with the projection[13]. For example, if someone projects Otherness onto me and I identify with the projection, I will feel out of place. If someone projects inferiority onto me and it sticks, I will feel inferior, or inadequate. As a result, the recipient of the projection experiences an intrusion into their psychic space. An intrusion into their psychological boundaries.

We can use colonialism as a frame to make sense of the opening scenario. The group response triggered a visceral response upon entry into a white space, and with it the suffocating sense of being excluded. Even in the absence of words, we can put the spotlight on dynamics that are often silenced. Firstly, there is that strong sense of déjà vu. We may relate it to colonial scripts or racist stereotypes such as the Black body as a trespasser or an oddity and therefore an object of scrutiny. Returning to a social psychology perspective on trauma and the group-level wounds that may be left on whole cultural or ethnic groups[14] can help us make sense of our ongoing collective struggle in naming and containing racism[15] and the anxiety that can arise from confronting white supremacy.

TRAUMA AND THE BODY

There is no doubt that trauma has devastating consequences for our physical health and makes us more vulnerable to chronic illnesses. The psychological and physical responses to adverse experiences and trauma make us prone to long-term physical health problems. Those with a history of trauma are about three times more likely to experience conditions such as irritable bowel syndrome, chronic pain and chronic fatigue syndrome[16]. Trauma, chronic stress and racism have also been linked to several health conditions including cardiovascular disease,[17] obesity[18], diabetes[19] as we will see now and vulnerability to cancer-related death[20].

The impact of chronic stress

Upon writing Chapter 2, Black Minds, I came to the realisation that the Black scholars who most influenced me and who dedicated their lives to combating the cancer that is racism had died of cancer. Fanon died of leukaemia in 1961. Feminist author Audre Lorde died of breast cancer in 1992. In 1987, author James Baldwin passed from stomach cancer. In 1998, civil rights activist Kwame Ture died of prostate cancer. I remember reading long ago that following the assassination of Dr Luther King, his autopsy revealed that although he was just 39 when he was killed, his heart had aged well beyond his years. He had the heart of a 60-year-old. Even at the time, it was thought the stress of fighting racism had taken its toll. White supremacy had worn out his heart. The symbolism of an illness or foreign body that invades us from outside in is a potent one. It mirrors the workings of anti-Blackness in society.

As far as cancer inequality goes, African Americans have the highest death rate and shortest survival rate of any racial/ethnic group in the US for most cancers[21]. In the UK, prostate cancer, the most common cancer in men, is two to three times more likely in Black men than their white counterparts. The death rate for Black men is twice as high. Black men also develop prostate cancer younger[22]. Black women's survival rate for any cancer is among the lowest.

There are serious biological consequences to racism and discrimination. These include a damaged immune system, chronic **inflammation** and premature cell ageing[23]. These have been linked to health inequalities. Cellular ageing refers to our cells' reduced ability to divide and proliferate. Cellular ageing occurs in all organisms with the passing of time, although environmental factors such as stress have been shown to cause cellular damage, and gradually cause loss of cellular functions and eventually cell death.

Telomeres are DNA sequences that are found at both ends of a chromosome. Each time a cell replicates, its telomeres become shorter until it eventually dies. Telomere length is correlated with chronological age and cumulative wear and tear, which is generally due to stress. Several studies have found that regardless of other health or socio-economic backgrounds, experiences of racism are linked to shorter telomeres and that the more frequent the experiences, the faster the shortening of telomeres. In other words, experiences of discrimination accelerate biological wear and tear[25,26].

Inflammation

Our body is designed to defend against pathogens – bacteria, viruses and substances that appear foreign and harmful – via our immune system. A pathogen is a biological agent that causes disease or illness. When we are exposed to a new pathogen, we produce what is called an inflammatory immune response. Cortisol, a potent anti-inflammatory that helps us fight inflammation, is produced. However, when we're exposed to stressors or threats, we also produce cortisol and experience fear or perceived threat to safety, status or wellbeing; the production of cortisol and other hormones in such situations is adaptive and promotes survival. It prepares our body for a fight-or-flight (or freeze) response.

However, chronic stress leads to hyper-physiological levels of cortisol, which is believed to reduce the effectiveness of cortisol to regulate both the inflammatory and immune responses. This is because it decreases tissue sensitivity to cortisol, leading to constant tissue breakdown and impairment of the immune system such as our immune response attacking our own cells, rendering those who experience chronic stress less able to fight off infections due to systemic inflammation and chronically elevated cortisol levels[26].

Racism (which is a chronic stressor) has been found to increase chronic inflammation among African Americans. Although inflammation is nature's way to protect organisms from threats to their health, high levels of inflammation impair our ability to respond to threats from the outside. They can promote heart attacks, neurodegenerative diseases and metastatic cancers. A study found that racism alone may account for 50% of the increased inflammation among African Americans[26]. Reducing chronic stress decreases inflammation in the body and associated cortisol levels, which may reduce the risk not only of us developing chronic diseases but also of dying younger[26,27]. In the US alone, at the time of writing, over 500,000 people have died of COVID-19, with Black people disproportionately impacted. Research in the UK has shown Black groups may be up to four times more likely to die of COVID-19 due to structural racism[28-30]. The physical impact of racism creates psychological trauma, which can be expected to, in turn, affect Black people's capacity to fight infections and lead to further deaths, thus more trauma[29].

MISTRUST AND NEGLECT

In the US, medical mistrust has been found to be associated with delays in African American men accessing routine health visits for blood pressure and cholesterol screenings[31,32]. Black men who report experiences of racism are much more likely to delay routine medical appointments overall. People who show more medical mistrust are much less likely to make use of preventative health interventions. The body–mind split is once more challenged[33,34]. Our communities know that the health inequalities that plague Black groups simply cannot be separated from racism. We also know that the body cannot thrive when the mind is under assault. Similarly, the mind cannot thrive when the body hurts.

Also as part of the picture: we see our doctors when our conditions are more advanced, often lethally so. These patterns have also been found irrespective of healthcare access and health insurance, and they exist in the UK where the use of healthcare services is free at the point of access. In this state of affairs, a mixture of structural racism, distrust of health services and intergenerational trauma is likely at play. Patterns of self-neglect are also a factor. If we have been harmed and abused, we are much more likely to relate to ourselves with contempt and violence and therefore to continue the cycle of abuse. There is ample evidence that suggests that trauma survivors are much more likely to self-harm, misuse substances, become reckless with their life and health, basically behave in self-destructive ways. Often this is to manage difficult emotions, to self-medicate or to cope with or distract oneself from the traumatic memories or experiences we can't escape from internally or externally. Self-harming behaviours can be a way of escaping pain. Sometimes too they are about rage-filled self-hate.

SUMMARY

1.

Racism hurts the Black body. Dr Bessel van der Kolk argues that our body keeps the score and that it continues to tell stories that we cannot articulate. No understanding of racism and racial trauma can ever be complete without an examination of physical manifestations. We therefore need to pay attention to the Black body.

2.

The legacy of colonialism 'entitles' white people to Black bodies: This can leave us vulnerable to boundary violations. Protecting our boundaries is important to protect ourselves from the harm of racism.

3.

Patterns of self-neglect need to be closely monitored: People who are poorly treated by society tend to treat themselves in similarly unkind ways. This may be interpreted as an internalisation of racism or displacement of anger and rage towards ourselves.

4.

Bodily and psychological experiences help us understand racism: racial violence is enacted through space, symbolically and non-verbally. The existence of an embodied racial (sub)consciousness and of racial bodily memory that are inseparable from our social and historical consciousness needs to be taken seriously.

5.

Trusting our body and treating it with kindness is an important step in reducing the harm of racial violence, particularly the more subtle bodily manifestations of racism.

In the next chapter, **RAISING BLACK CHILDREN**, we consider some of the challenges of parenting a child in the context of white supremacy and look more closely at the impact of racial trauma across generations.

RACE REFLECTIONS

The relationship between our environment and our body and the ways we may come to be harmed by racism physically is complex. This section gives you the opportunity to reflect and develop skills to help resist and protect your health and body from racism.

What have you found most troubling in this chapter?

You may want to explore your bodily responses, images and thoughts that came to you and explore what they might take you back to.
Please use the Race Reflections reflective model (p.207) to help you.

....

....

....

....

....

To recover from trauma it is important to connect and trust our body. Body-centred activities like deep breathing exercises help us regulate our internal states and restore and repair the connection between our minds and our bodies.

How does your body respond to experiences of racism? For some of us, it is our heart, or our stomach; for others, it is the head that holds the distress. Identifying where in our body we hold the racial distress can help us provide targeted relaxation. You could consider using an intentional soothing or healing touch for the areas you tend to tense while you practise some relaxation. Record your bodily response here.

....

....

....

....

....

We have seen that treating our body harshly or neglecting our physical health can be a reproduction of societal contempt, and that it can increase health inequality and the burden of disability and chronic health.

How do you tend to relate to your body? What tone of voice do you use? Think about the ways you might have been punishing, neglectful and/or abusive towards your body and what may need to change for you to have a more supportive relationship with your body.

....

....

....

....

....

We have seen that the Black body is vulnerable to becoming the repository of others' fantasies, fears and disowned material.

What bodily experience did you have that you now feel may be accounted for by you taking in other people's 'stuff'? Reflect on these experiences, and try to identify patterns. This will provide an opportunity for you to put psychological boundaries in place. Record your thoughts below.

....

....

....

....

....

ACTION POINT
CELEBRATE YOUR BODY

Knowing what you know about the Black body may trigger mixed emotions, and perhaps even a sense of grief for the ways in which you might have treated your body.

Your action point: Now that you have finished reading this chapter, start a new relationship with your body. You may find writing a letter to yourself helpful. As you write, you may find the following guidelines useful. Imagine that you are someone who loves everything about you deeply and unconditionally:

1. What might they say about your body?

2. What soothing words might they use to describe the part of yourself you dislike?

3. How might they encourage you to do better when it comes to how you have learnt to treat yourself?

4. What might they be proud of in relation to your body?

Once you build a picture of this person, try every day to be more like them until the distinction between you and them disappears.

CHAPTER 5

RAISING BLACK CHILDREN

When she was six my daughter came home upset and asked me to re-do her hair. She had gone to school with two pony-tails, two Afro puffs to be precise, and two cornrows at the front and two at the back of her head. She looked alarmed and anxious. 'The teacher said my hair is too big, I can't wear a hat and I need to change it, or I won't be in the school play,' she exclaimed. I reassured her. I said I would not change her hairstyle and that her hair was perfectly fine. The following day her father took her to school and explained to the teacher her comments were out of line and that she needed to be included in the school play whether her hair could fit into a hat or not. Furthermore, he showed her how to gather her Afro puffs into one to fit a hat. In the afternoon I picked her up and one of her braids at the back of her head had been cut. She had not realised. Only the teacher had touched her hair, to put it in a hat . . . I contacted the school; they had no idea. The head teacher wanted to double-check her braid had indeed been cut, in case I was mistaken, I presume. She agreed, then confirmed children had had no access to scissors. I explained to her the conflict around my daughter's Afro hair. I insinu-ated this may have been an act of malicious retaliation. The head teacher was outraged. She could not fathom that racism could be taking place in her school. This was beyond the realm of possibility. She disclosed to me that she had mixed-race grandchildren and since she herself as head teacher had grandchildren of colour who she loved very much, no racism could possibly be taking place in her school. We never found out who had cut my girl's hair. We never heard anything further either. This chapter tackles the challenges of raising Black children amid racism and racial trauma.

RAISING BLACK CHILDREN

We often say there is no manual that teaches you how to be a parent. That is certainly true. The aim of this chapter is not to provide a manual for parents on how to raise Black children. To a large extent, the task of raising Black children is the task of raising any children. We do the best we can with what we have and what we know. Nonetheless, in addition to general concerns around supporting Black children to become independent adults, the task of the Black parent is also to help their child navigate racism, and as far as is possible, to protect them from its harm. No blueprint to facilitate this overly complex task can ever exist. Black children are usually invisible from conversations around racism's traumatic effects. Few studies look at the impact of racism across a lifespan. This chapter aims to centre the needs of black children.

Black children start to become aware of race and racism at an incredibly young age. Our racialisation or socialisation to racial constructions as social beings starts early. By the age of three or four, children become aware of skin colour, or often much sooner. They start to understand racial categories, they show evidence of racial biases and preferences consistent with general societal attitudes. They begin to identify with one or several racial groups. By age four most are adept at recognising racial differences and what they signify for them. These may include awareness of the differential treatment they are afforded by people around them because of the colour of their skin. Children's racial socialisation is influenced by their parents' own experience of racism, racial attitudes and their coping or survival strategies[1]. Hence our child-rearing practices, identity, history and social positioning are, to a large extent, inseparable.

SCHOOL VIOLENCE

There is nothing more heart-breaking as a parent than leaving your child at a gate of a school knowing they will be subjected to racism and fearing that if you challenge the school they may be subjected to even more racism. Witnesssing their children experience racism can lead parents to racial trauma and/or activate memories of their own experience of racist violence in school or in other settings. Which then also has the potential to lead to further distress in children, leading to a cycle of wounding. That introductory extract at the start of the chapter is from an article I wrote in June 2019, 'On school, institutional racism and everyday violence'[1]. The article came about after I was heavily trolled on social media for suggesting that schools are as structurally and institutionally racist as the police and they are continuing, by and large, to get away with it. Teachers reacted defensively to my tweets to confirm they had never seen or experienced racism throughout their career. I wrote this piece to challenge their narrative but also to force many of those who refused to confront the realities of so many Black parents to see it. It is interesting that when publishing the piece, most, if not all, of those who were initially engaged in denial turned silent. Hundreds of messages followed, mainly from Black parents and parents of colour. Many shared their stories of racism in school.

It is concerning to me that even though what Black families experience is quite common[2], white people and schools continue to be shocked when we speak out. The inequalities in the school system have long been documented. We know that Black pupils:

- are two and-a half times more likely than white pupils to be mis-allocated to a lower set in maths, even if from higher socio-economic backgrounds.
- are routinely exposed to racial harassment, in the UK. And Brexit has led to a surge of racism and to

exclusions because of racism in primary schools in England going up by more than 40%.

- may be three times more likely to be affected by fixed-term exclusions and to be seen to be troublemakers.
- are being excluded because their natural hair is deemed inappropriate.

The above inequalities are the tip of the iceberg[3,4]. Schools are arguably a pillar of white supremacy and a site of trauma. This is what the expression 'school to prison pipeline'[5] seeks to highlight, that school policies and practices create conditions that increase the likelihood of social exclusion and later incarceration, to protect the dominance, superiority and privileges of white groups. So, what does it say to us as Black parents that when we reflect on racism, so many white teachers still feel the need to defend, argue and deny?

Influenced by Kwame Ture, late English judge William Macpherson defined institutional racism as 'the collective failure of an organisation to provide an appropriate and professional service to people because of their colour, culture or ethnic origin'. He further added that it can be seen in 'processes, attitudes and behaviour which amount to discrimination through unwitting prejudice, ignorance, thoughtlessness and racist stereotyping which disadvantages minority ethnic people'[6].

ABSENT DADS, BOSSY MUMS

There are enduring stereotypes about Black parenthood. The absent father is such a trope. And while this idea is heavily peddled within popular culture and political discourses both in the UK and the US, many have challenged this narrative with facts. For example, Josh Levs' 'No, Most Black Kids Are Not Fatherless'[7] challenged the myth using data from the US Centers for Disease Control and Prevention. It shows that most Black fathers do in fact live with their children (2.5 million versus 1.7 million who don't). And that regardless of living arrangements, Black fathers are among the most involved in the life of their children. So, where does this trope come from?

In 1965 a report by sociologist Daniel Patrick Moynihan titled *The Negro Family: The Case for National Action* was published. The report framed Black parents as the principal cause of an alleged culture of pathology within African American families. There was no attempt at identifying structural racism or other barriers that made mothering while Black challenging or the structural racism plaguing Black communities, even though the report pre-dates the end of the civil rights movement. It was argued that this work contributed to society seeing African American mothers as deficient, lacking and pathological[8].

In the UK researchers have found similar stereotypes to be pervasive too[9,10]. Following the fatal stabbing of a 14-year-old in 2012 as he stepped off a bus in London, Black British MP David Lammy made a controversial speech[11] calling for a more active form of fatherhood in the Black community. He argued that focusing on fathers was the key to tackling knife crimes in the capital. That it could help reduce educational 'under-achievement', disproportionate exclusion rates and high crime rates among Black youth. The major issue with Lammy's speech was that it was decontextualised and thus presented stereotypical narratives that have the power to do much more harm than good. It is correct, in the context of the UK, that Black children are more likely to live in unmarried households. However, non-traditional households do not necessarily translate to absent fathers or absent fathers to criminality. Such questionable conclusions paint Black fathers as irresponsible, immoral and unbothered by their children's welfare. Instead, in one of the largest reviews of youth knife crime, researchers found that adverse childhood experiences, poor mental health, discrimination and inequality are the main factors associated with youth violence.[12]

TALKING TO BLACK CHILDREN ABOUT RACISM

Racism is not the only challenge Black parents face, but it is one that cannot simply be ignored. Parents can be at a loss about how best to support their children when it comes to racist experiences. Should they have '**the talk**' or should they not, and if so, how? For way too many, it seems, this dilemma is resolved by not talking about racism at all. Or by delaying the conversation for as long as possible, often until the child is in their teens. Or even when the child reaches adulthood. Sometimes these conversations never happen. And although we can easily rationalise the upholding of silences, they result in Black children being left to manage the anxiety and distress that anti-Blackness creates without any guidance or support. They are therefore left vulnerable to racial trauma. 'The talk' is mainly an American cultural practice, born out of centuries of racial oppression on American soil. It is not clear how widespread the practice is outside of the US, but it appears to be less common.

To test that, I conducted a study with Black people before writing this chapter and asked research participants whether they had had a conversation about racism as children, and if so, what age they were when it occurred. Over 700 people engaged in the survey and it generated several conversations online. The broad trends of the survey were as follows:

- **AGE:** While more people reported being spoken to about racism (about 60%), about 40% said they did not have this conversation or that they did not remember having it. About 40% of those who had the conversation were 9–12.
- **ETHNICITY:** Differences across various Black groups came to light. Generally, Black people in the UK seem much less likely to talk to their children

about racism than Black people in the US, and Black African groups in the UK are much less likely to report having these conversations than Black Caribbean.

- **IMPLICATIONS:** Not discussing racism seriously disadvantages Black children. It affects awareness of and preparation for managing racist encounters, and deprives them of support. As we'll cover later, this denial has been linked to mental health challenges later in life.

ADVERSE CHILDHOOD EXPERIENCES

Trauma can happen at any age. Being told by a friend they are not allowed to play with us because we are Black. A teacher wrongly accusing us of cheating because we produced a piece of work deemed above our intellectual abilities. Being marked down or disciplined for completely arbitrary and subjective reasons, often because a teacher cannot fathom a gifted Black child, particularly when they are non-deferential and irreverent. Being discouraged from going to university. Being repeatedly punished more harshly at schools for similar infractions committed by white pupils. Additional common experiences include witnessing Black men being disproportionately stopped and searched by the police, hearing parents being racially abused, seeing loved ones being discriminated against. All this creates a context of chronic stress that can cumulatively have a traumatic effect on Black children and create a climate of **Adverse Childhood Experiences** (ACEs)[13]. ACE is the term used to describe distressing experiences that happen to us before we are 18, which have lifelong negative emotional and physical effects. ACEs are attracting increased scrutiny in public health because they have been found to be linked to health inequality between racial groups. For many parents, then, talking about racism to younger children can be a challenge.

This is something I experienced first-hand. After my mother and sister were horribly assaulted, after the screams, after the distress and terror, a deafening silence engulfed us all. We did not speak about the horror we had all witnessed. We of course spoke, but we did not talk as a family about racism. We did not talk about it as a community. Even at school, where everyone would have evidently heard about it, since so many children were present, silence reigned. My mother's face remained deformed for months. I can still see the white of one of her eyes tainted with blood. The family, the school and our community proceeded to behave as though nothing had happened. No one, it seemed, could put words onto the assault. We were all left to process this painful event together but alone and in silence. The perpetrator was jailed, and my mother's face and head slowly recovered. She regained her beauty. It was only several years after this incident that my mother broached the subject of racism with us. I think by then I was 9 or 10. It was decades after these initial conversations that as a family we broke the silence on the assaults. Over thirty years had passed. We had all remembered and forgotten different bits. This is what trauma does. It shatters memories and makes it difficult to put the pieces together. Nonetheless, as we made space for it, a collective memory started to emerge from the silence[14]. As we have seen, silence is often a sign of trauma,[15] of our capacity to make sense being overwhelmed by horror or fear. Or a sign that we would rather not speak into existence our experience, wish it did not take place. The ubiquity of silence following traumatic experiences became obvious in my work with various survivor groups, including survivors of sexual or gender-related violence, survivors of war and persecution and survivors of other forms of overwhelming experiences. This is a phenomenon that is well documented[16]. So much so it is often said that silence is the voice of trauma.

Case study: 'The school that tried to end racism'
In June 2020, Channel 4 launched a documentary series that followed year 7 pupils at a school in South London, Glenthorne High School, for three weeks[17]. The school ran an experiment aiming to tackle racial bias and racism. As part of the programme, conversations on race were encouraged in segregated groups and children were followed home to observe them share with their parents their reflections on the programme. In one episode, Bright, a young Black boy, returns home and discusses his experience of racism with his mother. He fidgets and looks ill at ease, rarely making eye contact with her. At times he seems to stutter. We see him on the verge of tears as he tries to find the words to communicate to his mother his experience of being repeatedly stopped and searched and racially profiled by the police, despite his young age.

Bright seems to be in his early to mid-teens. He is obviously smart and understands he is the victim of racism. He is confident outside of this exchange. As he speaks, his mother watches him, also looking somewhat ill at ease as he says: 'Whenever you go into a shop you feel like, "oh hopefully I don't get stopped today," and it just gets to you'. She is initially silent but appears to be listening intently. Then her response to Bright leaves the audience feeling something is disjointed; she exclaims, 'this is based on what has happened before, the shopkeeper is not lying, and you should not be angry.' In her attempt to comfort Bright, the mother rationalises the racism and invalidates Bright's experience. Bright becomes more agitated as he continues to struggle to be heard.

PARENT–CHILD CONFLICTS

This scene is gut-wrenching. Many found it upsetting and took to social media to voice their distress both at Bright's regular experience of racism and at his mother's response. Others were quick to criticise her and connected to Bright's struggle to be understood. My heart broke for Bright, but I also felt compassion towards his mother. Based on her accent, my impression is that she is a West African migrant. She is a mother who was attempting to manage the racist experiences her child brings home, while probably being unprepared. A mother who appears disconnected from her son's lived reality. A mother who inadvertently silences to soothe.

Bright's mother is not alone in struggling and neither is he. They are both struggling, but each one alone. In the UK and through both my research and clinical work on racial trauma, that very same struggle often features. For most people I come across, there is little evidence of having had 'the talk'.

Where immigration is concerned, important differences can exist in terms of worldview between parents and their children simply due to age, generation and diaspora. The Black British population is primarily composed of descendants of immigrants from the Caribbean and Africa who in the main migrated to the UK after the Second World War. Today according to the last ONS census, Black residents in the UK make up about 3% of the country's population but 13% of those are born abroad[18]. In the UK 95% of Black Africans arrived after 1981 whereas for Black Caribbean groups the percentage was 61%. The fact that Black Caribbean families have been coping with white supremacy in Britain for longer than Black Africans may translate into them being better able to articulate British racism.

These patterns of migration matter a great deal in the context of Blackness in Britain. They are often amplified by broader histories of displacement, alienation and colonial violence. For a significant large number of Black families, one or both parents may not have been born in Britain or Europe. Perhaps they might have immigrated from the Caribbean or from Africa. And while there is absolutely no doubt that white supremacy is a global phenomenon operational at a geopolitical level, meaning it exists across nations and is deeply ingrained in the fabric of former colonies, parents' racial politics and experiences of racism may be very different to those of their children. These differences may lead to the kind of conflicting exchanges we witnessed in 'the school that tried to end racism' case study.

Stories of migration and experiences of racism are vastly different across the diaspora. They depend on the host countries or how recent the migration is, and, of course, the historical context. We do know that migration and displacement cause multiple challenges for Black family units alongside the usual difficulties of raising children. Not least mental health. Migrant groups' vulnerability to psychological distress is well documented by decades of research[19, 20, 21]. There are many factors that account for that vulnerability: The loss of familiarity and social networks. Racialised xenophobia. In the UK, the Windrush scandal comes to mind. Black people are a growing segment of the immigrant population in the United States. Although discourses around migration in the US are centred around people from South and Central America, the number of Black migrants to the US is rising sharply. In 1980 there were 816,000 Black immigrants, 2.4 million in 2010 and 4.2 million in 2016. Currently, it is estimated that about 10% of the Black population in the United States was born outside of the country.

Undocumented Black migrants are also more likely to be over-policed, incarcerated or deported[22]. 76% of Black immigrants are deported on criminal grounds, compared to 45% of all immigrants. This is the result of hostility, the stigma and marginalisation encountered in the country. Social deprivation and/or economic challenges can also lead to or exacerbate racial trauma. This trauma often echoes traumatic violence experienced in the country of origin, particularly for forced migrants. Sometimes parents who are migrants and have left persecutory contexts may not be prepared to listen to criticisms related to the new country because of a need to idealise their new home in order to feel safe and justify the major life changes immigration has brought. They may simply not have the emotional capacity to cope with additional trauma.

Generational differences have a deep impact. Research suggests, for example, that the so-called second generation of migrants are much more aware of the reality of racial injustice. They are less assimilative in their aspiration and more vocal about their entitlement to justice and equal treatment. This makes sense if we consider that older generations may not necessarily consider Britain or the 'host country' as their new home, but a temporary place of abode. A place primarily to work with a view to returning 'back home' to retire. Similarly, parents may feel that their offspring's struggle of everyday racism do not compare with their own struggles. Especially in cases where parents have experienced persecution, torture, extreme poverty or colonial racism. They may inadvertently minimise their children's difficulties. A communication gap may start to emerge that can have profound implications for the quality of parent–child relationships. It can alienate children and foster further silence. For all these reasons, migrants' families often experience relational difficulties[23].

ATTACHMENT AND HISTORICAL BONDS

Slavery and enslavement have also left enduring marks on **attachment**. Attachment is the bond between a child and their caregivers, particularly the mother. It was British psychologist and psychoanalyst John Bowlby who initiated clinical interest in attachment[24]. He described attachment as a 'lasting psychological connectedness between human beings.' This connectedness is an evolutionary mechanism to ensure the survival of the species that he suggested had a huge impact on the child's mental health, lasting well into adulthood.

American-Canadian psychologist Mary Ainsworth examined children's responses to being (artificially) separated from their caregivers[25]. The level of anxiety and distress they displayed, as well as their responses when reuniting with the caregiver, was found to be a reliable source of information to assess the nature of the bond that exists between them. A 'secure' attachment helps the child to begin to develop abstract or symbolic 'mastery'. In time, as the infant internalises the soothing attention and care they receive when in need, they learn to tolerate distress without undue dread. This helps them to later feel safe and trusting in intimate relationships. There is a great deal of research on attachment within the field of psychology, most of which is premised on the idea that the first relationship, usually with our mother, shapes our internal configurations and becomes an enduring relational template that we use to manage relationships and know what to expect in the world.

The attachment bond is shaped by the way in which the infant responded to early relational experiences. An infant, whose distress is contained, and whose needs are cared for, learns to trust both their internal world and the world around them. Feeling contained, nurtured and safe is essential for optimal cognitive development. Feeling secure helps us think.

A few fundamental characteristics of slavery bear direct relevance when considering attachment, and in Black groups particularly those who are direct descendants of enslaved Africans. For centuries, on the continent millions saw loved ones kidnapped or sold away overnight[26]. Once in the Americas being enslaved meant living under the constant threat of separation. Children could be sold away at an instant's notice. Enslaved women were rarely afforded time to bond with their infants since they were expected shortly after giving birth to return to the fields. Dissociating from the pain of separation was necessary to survive.

Attachment challenges are amplified by immigration. The ease with which Black African and Black Caribbean parents can leave children behind via immigration, the dissociation from the distress this causes, does not only speak of punishing economic realities and geopolitical inequalities, but also says something about the normalisation of disrupted attachment, of separation and the numbing of distress. The collective violence our ancestors were subjected to. The survival strategies they perfected to keep alive have not completely disappeared, far from it, and they continue to affect family dynamics such as causing conflicts, resentment or envy between siblings when some were left behind 'back home' and others were born in or brought to the West. Although we can sometimes fool ourselves into believing that these times are far behind us today, in the history of modern civilisation Black groups have spent more time enslaved and colonised than they have spent time free.

INTERNALISED RACISM

We usually speak of internalised racism[27] to refer to the way people of colour accept the veracity of the white supremacy as ideology and inevitably the notion of their inherent inferiority. It is when we take actions that reproduce the system of racism. We can see internalised racism in our preference for lighter-skinned individuals and the hierarchy we uphold around skin shade so that many of us hold in higher regards those with proximity to whiteness. We can see internalised racism in our veneration of white European cultures, values and worldviews. We can see internalised racism in our drive to assimilate and aim to resemble or sit next to the master. Some see internalised racism as one of the most common, yet least studied, features of racism. The subject is fraught with taboo, shame and avoidance, leading to many misconceptions and unmet psychological needs. Most Black people have learnt that we need to be twice as good as our white counterparts to be deemed good enough to stand underneath them. Similarly, it is not unusual for Black parents to mirror (consciously or otherwise) the harsh treatment society metes out to Black boys. To respond with a punishing rhetoric to any lapse in conduct, particularly those associated with racial prejudices, out of fear that negative societal expectations and the dreaded stereotypes may materialise. This 'double bind' can be used to make sense of internalised racism. It refers to the illusionary and implicit promise by white structures that Black people can escape the consequences of their Otherness by disowning their 'difference'. Their Blackness.

Clearly internalised racism cannot be separated from issues of intergenerational trauma and issues of identification with the aggressor. A kind of Stockholm Syndrome, some may say, can take place, where we feel compelled to identify with, relate to and emulate those who harm to gain power and control. We may, therefore, link this double bind to the double consciousness[28], seeing ourselves through our eyes but also through the eyes of white people. All communities internalise the dominant beliefs of society and therefore the expression as exclusively applied to people of colour is misleading. However, if staying silent means racism is not confronted and the status quo is maintained, then staying silent when harmed by racism is also a manifestation of internalised racism. But achieving the promise of the double bind is impossible. Audre Lorde believed that silence does not protect us. It cannot protect us because racism remains the operative system whether we name it or not. Its damage continues.

PARENTAL TRAUMA

It is difficult to put into words how difficult it is for many of us to deal with schools. I have repeatedly said that handling race-based conflicts within schools is one of the most difficult experiences to navigate as a Black mother. There is undoubtedly a triggering effect. When we have experienced racism at schools ourselves, seeing our children also experience it can be extremely distressing. So of course, the temptation is to avoid facing things that remind us of our own experience or trauma. Furthermore, the availability and quality of support children are provided with will also be affected by their parents' experiences of racism at the time.

Chronic or severe stress, as we have seen, can have far-reaching consequences on the body, but it also affects family functioning[29]. It can affect closeness, patience and availability. In some cases, chronic stress in parents can even lead to abuse and neglect. The chronicity of racism poses serious challenges to Black family units. It means that often as the child faces racism at school one or both of their parents may also be struggling with racism at work or at university for example. If so, their emotional responsiveness to the child may well be compromised. When we are preoccupied with any racial injustices happening to us and we face chronic discrimination ourselves, our capacity to be there for our children can suffer[30, 31]. In turn, children may learn that they should not 'burden' an emotionally stretched parent. They will pick up cues on how the parent responds or speaks. We may well be unconsciously telling children we do not have capacity to hear.

PROTECTING BLACK CHILDREN

Black parents sometimes uphold silences or dismiss racism consciously seeking to protect their children. Similarly, in my own research, participants often believed their parents were attempting to protect them. Protect their innocence, protect them from having distressing conversations but, of course, that is not the whole story. Many may be convinced speaking will damage their children. That it will make children less able to function within white supremacy or cause them to lose ambition or confidence in themselves. I believe this was the case in my home when I was growing up. My parents believed that we were too young to understand. Too young to face and deal with the terror of whiteness. They also placed high value on education. They would have done anything to protect our aspirations. Their silence, I am certain, was also born out of the desire not to discourage us. They wanted so badly to protect our life chances.

But the reality is we were never fully protected. It was never within their gift to protect us from white supremacy. Black parents do not have that power. We saw the differing treatment, the attitudes towards our parents. We heard their stories when they got home after work exhausted and complained about mundane acts of injustice and discrimination. And of course, we experienced racism directly too. Silence may be employed to protect parents from having to connect to feelings of powerlessness when it comes to the ability to safeguard their children from racism. It protects them from the hopelessness to see one's child experience the same traumas their ancestor they or did. This possibly explains in some the wish to delay for as long as possible the need to face it all. Children also often keep silent about their racist experiences, sometimes out of shame, often wanting to protect their parents by sparing them additional hurt and pain.

LANGUAGE AND SELF-CARE

One of the main reasons Black children need language and strategies to manage experiences of racism is because they are at risk of internalising negative stereotypes. Thus, to be deprived of the opportunity to forge a sense of who they are, beyond what society and those around them may think and project onto them. All children are vulnerable to believing that they deserve or are responsible for mistreatment and violence that is done to them. Black children are no different. Silence fosters self-hate and breeds shame. A major task in therefore supporting children and equipping them with what they need to build a positive racial identity is giving them strategies to externalise what is put onto them within a racist society.

When Black children are not given tools to deal with negative messages they receive from others, their ideas of who they are will be constructed of combinations of environmental and societal discourses. These include stereotypes and negative expectations acquired from school and the media. Black children receive both covert and overt messages that tell them that they are intellectually deficient, frequently from teachers' biases[32].

We cannot expect optimal cognitive development while we fail to support Black children with their experience of racism. The consequence of racism is often **anxiety**. Anxiety impairs our ability to learn, to concentrate and retain information. Silence and the denial of racism by parents have been shown to amplify anxiety[33]. When a child experiences a trauma in a context where they have been taught they cannot trust or rely on their parents or carer for support, the world can suddenly seem very scary. Dangers and fears are often exaggerated as children attempt to fill blanks with what they do not understand or know. In silence, the child gets the message that there is something that is dreadful, unspeakable, that it is beyond the ability of the parent to help them with. In time they might learn that support cannot come from their loved ones. So not only is racism something we do not talk about, it is something we struggle with alone. Something not worth seeking support for. By extension, the message is that they will face incomprehensible experiences and that no one will be here to help.

These expectations and relational patterns can be taken into adulthood and affect intimacy, security and safety in relationships and in the world more generally. Finally, keeping harm silent is not processing it. What is not processed is not healed. Many psychologists say that what a generation cannot bear, tends to be passed on to burden the next generation. So, silence may well support the transmission of intergenerational trauma, continuing to feed the circle of harm. The fact is that our fears are often amplified by the silence that surrounds us. Naming them and facing our discomfort can help us make space for these conversations.

SUMMARY

1.

Silence is all too often the response, the main survival or coping strategy after trauma: The complexities of supporting Black children, especially while parents themselves may be struggling with experiences of racism or with their own unprocessed trauma, needs much attention.

2.

Silence is reproduced by society: Within the psychology and mental health scholarship, the literature is thin. Parents and children are therefore left unsupported, a symptom itself of systemic racism. In that system, those who speak out and challenge racism can face punishment, discredit and/or violence.

3.

If silence is forcefully enforced by society and has a long history, it is not something we can hold Black parents solely responsible for: Yet, as Black parents we can do better. There is so much we cannot bear to face. There is so much we would rather not hear too. Partly because it takes us to our own painful histories.

4.

Racism will not be the only challenge Black families will need to negotiate: Of course, social deprivation is another factor for many, as is the intersection of migration-related challenges. This will greatly increase the level of stress a family is exposed to and impact their emotional availability and attachment. Silence is simply not an option.

In the next chapter, **WORKING WHILE BLACK**, we look at what it is like to navigate white workplaces as a Black employee, some of the ways racism manifests at work and what we can do to support ourselves.

RACE REFLECTIONS

We saw that racism causes many challenges to the family unit and can affect our relationships with children. We need to tackle these challenges head on to safeguard Black children's welfare. This section gives you the opportunity to reflect and develop skills to help resist and protect Black children from racism.

What have you found most troubling in this chapter?

You may want to explore your embodied responses, images and thoughts that came to you and explore what they might take you back to. Please use the Race Reflections reflective model (p.207) to help you.

....

....

....

....

....

What have been your parents' and grandparents' formative experiences of racism? What stories of theirs have stayed with you?

What do you think they might have passed on to you about the world and how do they relate to your fears? What has been helpful and what has been less helpful? What might you want to pass on to younger generations and what would you rather leave behind?

....

....

....

....

....

What are your key fears when it comes to racism and how do they manifest?

It is important that you connect with potential fears and name them so they do not 'leak' into your relationship with your child/children. Our fears can manifest in many ways such as in overprotection or under-protection, in harshness or invalidation; please be curious about how your fears may manifest.

....

....

....

....

....

When it comes to conversations about racism with children, what could you do better?

Reflect on the conversations you have had with younger Black people; what could you do differently to make them more supportive and validating? If you have not had these conversations, consider what you might need to feel more comfortable having them. On the next page, you will find tips on having these discussions.

....

....

....

....

....

TALKING TO BLACK
CHILDREN ABOUT RACISM

A couple of things before you start . . .

Prepare emotionally

This may be both the simplest and the most difficult thing to do.

It can be extremely difficult to confront racism as a parent. It may take us back to our own experience of racism and oppression. It may make some of us feel that we have somehow failed as a parent. Feelings of helplessness, powerlessness and/or guilt about not having been able to shelter the child from the reality of oppression may arise. Some parents may even feel angry the child is responding in a way that they may see as 'unhelpful'.

A range of feelings and emotions may be evoked, which will be picked up by the child. A lack of preparation could lead us to invalidate the child's experience, or it could derail the conversation, distract, make us change the subject, or laugh things off.

Please resist. Silencing the child may assign shame to their experience and/or teach them that the subject is taboo or could cause offence, embarrassment or hurt to you. Consequently, the child may not bring the subject up again and may learn instead to keep this potentially troubling experience to themselves. Silencing the child might even reinforce any potential association between themselves, Blackness and being 'bad'.

Engage on the child's level

Try to remain curious and open so you can meet the child where the child is at.

Probe the child with open and neutral questions so that you can start to build a picture of their experience and belief system such as the qualities that have been attributed to Blackness and whiteness. Ask your child how they make sense of experiences they may bring to you. But also, be on the look-out for belief around responsibility and feelings of shame. If you start where your child is at, you will be better able to challenge problematic beliefs in due course and to provide relevant counter-narratives.

Part of engaging the child where they are at is remembering the child's age. Having a conversation with a five- or six-year-old is different from having a conversation with a 14-year-old. There is no need to expose younger children to violent, brutal or graphic images or conversations that will likely increase their anxiety. But similarly downplaying what teenagers are exposed to on social media or at school will not help build trust or meet the child's need.

Remember: balance matters

We can easily become preoccupied with racism, particularly when we are at the receiving end of it.

While this is understandable it may lead us to overdo it when it comes to talking about racism. Please bear that in mind. It is also important that we remember that our behaviour will have much more of an impact than our words. The way we respond to racism will teach children how to respond to racism. Similarly, how we treat children will teach them about how to expect to be treated in the world. There is a balance to be struck: by over-focusing on racism, on abuse and on trauma-loaded conversations, we may do more harm than good.

So, it is important to help children connect with joy and beauty too. Being loved, nurtured and attended to are probably the strongest buffers against racial trauma and help internalise safety. It is important to teach Black children that they are loved and that they are lovable and that they matter. This is arguably the most important message in fostering self-love.

10 TOP TIPS

1. **Start with thanking the child for their openness and courage.** This is important to reinforce the idea that your child was right to come to you and that you will be there whenever they experience racism and other difficult or confusing situations.
2. **Learn about child development** in relation to challenging conversations on racism. Some may find therapeutic support helpful, others may be satisfied with doing their own research.
3. **Take the initiative.** Do not wait for the child to be 'old enough' to start thinking about such conversations. It is also not helpful to wait for them to bring up racism. Your child may well be waiting for you to signal that it is okay to start the conversation, or they may want to protect you!
4. **Give yourself permission to grieve.** The most important part of preparing for conversations on racism is to allow yourself to grieve and be upset by the reality that you will likely have to help your child navigate anti-Blackness.
5. **Be reflective.** A central part of preparation is to be reflective around our own fears and our own experiences to try not to project them onto the child. Carry out some of the exercises in Chapter 5 and Chapter 1.
6. **Seek support.** Beforehand and afterwards. It is completely understandable to feel uncertain and worried; some preparation will stop you from feeling completely out of your depth. Who else can you discuss these experiences with? Is there another parent and family member who could offer reassurance and help you find the right words? Remember to look after your wellbeing too if your child is the victim of racism.
7. **Create a Black-centric home.** It is crucially important that Black children have access to positive role models who look like them. This environment signals to children that Blackness matters and that Blackness is beautiful. This will also help with the development of a more secure cultural identity and a healthy self-esteem. Further, art, books and other cultural products provide opportunities for parents to start to talk about history and racism in their own terms as opposed to being thrown in at the deep end because of a racist incident at school, for example.
8. **Show unconditional love** to your child before, during and after the conversation. It is easy for parents to assume that their children know

they are loved. But research suggests many adults never felt loved as children. It is absolutely vital that the context within which the conversations on racism take place is a context where the child feels loved because this will challenge racist messages and the hostile or hateful language or incidents you may need to discuss. Attentiveness, availability, kindness, compassion and tone are often what children use to assess love.

9. **Create safety.** As much as it is within your power, ensure your home and your relationship are safe when you are preparing to have a conversation about racism. Can you have it in a place and room where your child feels safe? Can you support your child with feeling as safe as possible after the conversation? Black children can benefit from basic relaxation and self-soothing skills.

10. **Do not sweat it**! Trust yourself as a parent. If you are attentive, seek to build your capacity and develop like most parents do, you are likely to become a good-enough parent to a Black child.

ACTION POINT
STRENGTHEN YOUR BONDS

This chapter's action point is focused on strengthening attachment within the family. Connection and solid bonds act as protection from toxic environments. They also communicate to us that we are worthy of love, care and attention, and encourage a child to feel safe enough to come to you with their distress.

We can all improve the quality of our bonds if we commit ourselves to doing so. Connection relies on first and foremost making time for bonding. It relies on seeing and hearing the Other and tapping into our capacity to show compassion to one another, including towards children. Human touch, eye contact and active listening help most children feel contained. Make a connection action plan with your children, niblings and other little humans around. Ensure that you regularly engage with the focus of connecting and making them feel heard and seen.

CHAPTER 6

WORKING WHILE BLACK

Case study: Sara
Sara is a Black British woman of Caribbean heritage in her early thirties who works as a manager in the civil service. Sara had been experiencing severe anxiety, debilitating shame and difficulties working with her manager. Sara's manager is a white man and she seemed to have developed a 'phobic' response or extreme fear towards him. Sara frequently found herself advocating for less senior employees of colour who faced discrimination. This added much tension in her relationship with management. She essentially became the voice of racism, thus the 'troublemaker'. She was treated with hostility and regularly covertly disrespected. Sara was finding the workplace increasingly oppressive and often ended up in tears. She was hopeless and overwhelmed when I spoke to her, during an assessment. Exploring the relationship between Sara and her manager and the workplace as a structure formed a significant part of our work together. Of note, Sara had a history of being bullied, including racial harassment in her childhood, and had been the carer for her widowed father, as he spent most of her life in and out of severe depression.

We know that all organisations nowadays take equality 'very seriously'. Yet we also know that Sara's experience is far from uncommon. In fact, I am still to meet a single Black employee who has not faced a backlash for speaking out against racism.

To understand the lived experience of working while Black, various less discussed manifestations of anti-Blackness will be explored and linked to some of the themes we have been grappling with so far. Black experiences at work cannot be separated from historical contexts. We therefore need to revisit the relationship between white spaces and Black bodies. These links will help us better appreciate some of the risks we commonly face and the strategies we can put in place to mitigate them. In this chapter we aim to make connections and reflect on common experiences of working while Black and also how the injustices and injuries that can be sustained in the workplace not only mirror wider social inequality but also histories of trauma.

The 'Diversity and Inclusion' industry – if not the 'Diversity and Inclusion' industrial complex – is worth billions. In the US alone companies spend over eight billion dollars on D&I training each year[1]. While billions are spent on 'Diversity and Inclusion', Black graduates are still significantly less likely to find full-time jobs after graduating[2]. A recent study found that among young people who left university in 2017/18, 53% of the Black graduates had secured full-time employment, compared with 62% of white graduates[3]. What's more, a study by the Trade Union Congress found that they get paid 23% less when they do find employment and this gap widens as qualification increases. The list of inequality is long and, it would almost appear, never-ending. Inequalities at the point of access, inequalities in relation to progress and inequalities in relation to discipline, to name but a few.

In all Western nations where data is collected, Black people continue to experience hostile workplaces. These structural injustices are not reducing; in fact, in some places they are getting worse[4]. While all this structural context is known, what is less understood is the lived reality of negotiating it, the more subtle and complex dynamics that can reproduce the wider system and how the Black body is treated within white workplaces.

The D&I industry's love affair with **unconscious bias** has done extraordinarily little to make workplaces less discriminatory places for Black people. It is arguably doing more harm than good by taking the focus away from structural racism and from more complex unconscious dynamics. So, I am starting this chapter on three premises: Firstly, that workplaces are a microcosm of society and that every dynamic and process that occurs between and within groups in society will get mirrored within institutions. Secondly, that organisations as organisms generally do not want to change and will resist change in various and elaborate ways, regardless of what they may tell themselves. A Black body inhabiting a previously all-white space is a fundamental change that can and will often be resisted in various ways. Some more obvious than others. The final premise is related to both points, and it is that there is a level of communication, which is unseen and unconscious or pre-verbal, that neither Black employees, white employers nor structures are adequately equipped for or willing to explore. It is often at this level of interaction that most race-related conflicts, tensions and difficulties arise between Black employees and white institutions.

THE BLACK BODY AT WORK

Experiences of racism at work usually revolve around a main trope or script. The story often sounds like 'one of those stories' you have heard many times before and it usually has a firm déjà vu quality. This déjà vu quality is there because these experiences evoke past events and configurations and therefore need a historical lens to be understood. As we have seen, colonialism is the antithesis of personal sovereignty and boundary. I have therefore used the term micro-colonialism to refer to the everyday intrusions and breaches of boundaries, physical or psychological, such as invasions of privacy or personal space, Black people continue to experience within white spaces, particularly from white men but not exclusively from them. These experiences are also gendered and subject to intersectional considerations. For example, one common gendered boundary violation concerns the policing of Black hair.

Case study: Black hair

In 2019, Lettia McNickle of Quebec successfully sued her employer Madisons New York Bar and Grill after being told to leave work because she was wearing braids. The restaurant was ordered to pay $14,500 in damages[5]. There are plenty of examples of Black people in North America, particularly Black women, being punished for refusing to assimilate into whiteness via their hair. These assimilation orders are often rationalised under the guise of professionalism, uniform and grooming policies at work. Celebrities like Gabrielle Union have shared their experience of having their hair policed within the entertainment industry and being told that their hair was 'too Black' for a show or a particular audience. But this is not a showbiz-specific issue. Nor is it an issue that only affects Black (North) Americans.

In the UK, cases of Black women being excluded or suspended from work on the basis of their hair frequently make the headlines too. In 2017, a Black woman alleged that she was told while applying for a job at Harrods that she would be required to relax, which is to chemically straighten, her hair, in order to be accepted for employment in the UK luxury store. The case ended up in front of UK parliamentarians. There is no specific legislation in the UK banning hair discrimination, although there have been successful litigated cases linking hair to either race or religious belief. There is limited protection throughout the Western world from hair discrimination.

The 'CROWN' act 9, Creating a Respectful and Open Workplace for Natural Hair, was added to the California Education Code and the Fair Employment and Housing Act in 2019. On top of accepting a definition of race that includes traits associated with a particular racial group, including hair texture and hairstyles, it rendered hair discrimination unlawful. California is the first state to ban discrimination against natural Black hairstyles such as cornrows, Afros, braids and dreadlocks.

Although it has since been adopted beyond California, The CROWN act is one of the very few legal protection frameworks that exist in the world to protect against discrimination on the grounds of hair. This is even though we know Black people and particularly Black women continue to face stereotypes, exclusion and discipline because of the hair that grows out of their head. We now have evidence that wearing 'natural' hairstyles leads to perception of lack of professionalism and there are high penalties in terms of job opportunities for those who refuse to straighten their hair or style it in a way that makes it look as close to 'European' hair as possible[6].

Black women's hair texture and style continues to attract uninvited curiosity, intrusive questions, gazes and touch[7]. Although there is a tendency to trivialise such exoticisation, the history of Black hair within white supremacy is deep and fiercely political. And again, it is a history we cannot separate from colonialism and imperialism. The texture of Afro hair, for example, was used as 'justification' for the enslavement of Africans between the 16th and 19th centuries. When a white hand without our consent gets into our hair, it is the history of being objectified and bestialised that is re-enacted. The history of the animal zoo. The history of entitlement to the Black body and the associated breaches of boundary.

BEING 'THE ONLY ONE'

To be a Black professional often means to be the only one in meetings, departments and sometimes within whole organisations. High status roles and places of power in society remain overwhelmingly white[8]. Black people have not, by and large, benefitted from diversity programmes, or at least nowhere near the same level as white women and other people of colour have[9]. The road to leadership and a senior role is an arduous one and, if we get there, we must contend with the experience of being the only Black face around. It is interesting that when I reflect on my clinical work with professionals of colour the experience of being the only one is usually the one that carries the most distress or anguish, often beyond experiences of overt discrimination.

Being the only one carries significant psychological risks and can set off complex dynamics including that of the white gaze, and scapegoating. The lack of racial representation is central to our experience in the workplace; not seeing oneself represented at work is thus a foundational experience for many of us. Beyond organisational loss in terms of talent and innovation there is also a loss, and specifically a sense of grief, for Black workers. It often translates into individuals struggling with belonging and homeness, themes as we have seen in Chapter 2 that are deeply evocative of historical trauma. White institutions may go out of their way to recruit 'BME and Black candidates' or to attract 'difference', and so while once such (racial) difference enters the workplace, if it does at all, the expectation is usually that it must dress itself in whiteness. This rule is as powerfully as it is silently enforced. It is that very rule which dictates that we must remain silent when subjected to racism, that we must adapt, that we must overlook microaggressions and generally that we must keep white people comfortable.

THE IMPACT OF STEREOTYPES

In 1997, while assessing maths performance, researcher Steven Spencer found that when women were exposed to messages indicating that women perform as well as men on the test, they scored similarly to men[10]. When they were not, they scored more poorly on average than men. A few years later, similar results were found when assessing African American students[11]. Black students who were exposed to negative stereotypes about intelligence, for example, performed worse than those who were not. Today we have many studies that document the same effect and the dynamic has been given a name: stereotype threat[12]. There are various ways to make sense of these findings. Researchers have suggested that negative stereotypes lead those stereotyped to fear confirming the veracity of the feared stereotypes. To worry about their own performance, which might divert attention away from the task, compromising intellectual or cognitive performance. In that line of thought, stereotype threat is fear or anxiety of confirming stereotypes while taking a test.

There are, of course, various other ways to make sense of findings on stereotype threats, yet explanations for the phenomenon remain primarily theoretical. We may propose that we get discouraged or dispirited at being confronted with material that reminds us of racial injustice. Perhaps this affects our motivation to do well. We may also suggest that we identify with the stereotypes and therefore feel unconsciously pressured to act in accordance with them; this suggestion supports the dynamic of projective identification.

The impact of stereotypes on our cognitive or intellectual performance reminds us of how potent social forces can be in our psychological world and how such forces may come to influence how we are evaluated and/or how we respond to evaluation of our performances in work settings. Projective identification is an important dynamic for anyone serious about understanding race and the reproduction of inequality. Furthermore, it is a helpful tool for Black people to make sense of experiences we might have struggled to put into words. It provides us with a framework to take seriously our embodied responses in racialised exchanges and to consider what they might tell us about our personal sovereignty, but also about our political sovereignty.

IMPOSTER SYNDROME

In this context is it not obvious that many of us would struggle with self-doubt and confidence when it comes to our competence? Or that we may come to experience imposter syndrome? **Imposterism** or **imposter syndrome** has been taken to refer to internal feelings of fraudulence or incompetence[13]. Those who are said to experience imposter syndrome perceive themselves to be less deserving of their achievements or roles, and believe that others overestimate their abilities. Because of this discrepancy in terms of how they view themselves and how they are viewed by others, sufferers fear being discovered as a fraud. Although the original research on the phenomenon focused on white women, we now know that Black people face unique stressors and that again, racial stereotypes lie at the centre of their experiences. The lack of racial representation can activate internalised racism, which alone is associated with poor self-esteem and lack of confidence.

Assimilation for us is a complex process. Of course, there is a level of assimilation in the workplace that every employee regardless of their race and ethnicity must accept. Beyond this, there is, for Black employees, an additional level of labour that often goes unrecognised and is completely normalised. Another level of assimilation is racial and cultural – it's the expectation that Black people leave their Blackness at the door to get in, that they whiten themselves to be accepted by their peers or to not face barriers in relation to promotion.

This sort of assimilation is all-encompassing. It includes (but also goes much beyond) how our hair is worn. It includes not discussing our lived experience (particularly that of racism) and adopting modes of communication that may be alien to us to get ahead. So powerful is the expectation that we must leave our Blackness behind that many of us adopt a whole different persona, mannerisms, accent and sometimes language to fit in at work, a process many refer to as 'code switching'. The term was coined by US sociolinguist John J. Gumperz to refer to polyglots switching between languages and ended being applied onto how Black Americans learn to switch from standard English to **African American Vernacular English** (**AAVE**). Imagine going to work and having taught yourself for years, if not decades, to lead such an inauthentic life and fear being found out. Imagine the emotional demand, the exhaustion and alienation. Many of us do not have to imagine.

EXCELLENCE, EXHAUSTION
AND RESPECTABILITY

Many of us grow up in houses where narratives such as 'work harder', 'be smarter', are repeatedly enacted. 'You have to be twice as good'. Twice as good as everyone else and certainly twice as good as your white equivalent to simply be deemed good enough to stand underneath them. There is no doubt that part of these narratives originates from racial trauma and our intergenerational baggage; still our parents were not entirely incorrect. There is plenty of evidence that suggests that Black people, regardless of our sector, are more likely to be bypassed for promotion or recruitment even when they are the stronger candidates. The strategy of working twice as hard has heavy costs for our health and mental health as we have seen in Chapter 2. It can lead to perfectionism, anxiety and burnout. This is because the strategy of working twice as hard can increase our vulnerability to experiencing a kind of stress that psychologists sometimes refer to as **goal-striving stress**. Goal-striving stress is occasioned by the discrepancy that exists between aspirations and achievement, particularly when our constant striving to achieve does not lead to the outcome we seek. Research[14] indicates that goal-striving stress is associated with lower levels of happiness, life satisfaction and self-esteem and higher levels of psychological distress.

This same process has been termed '**John Henryism**'. The empirically documented health impact of 'high-effort coping' we sometimes put in place to attempt to overcome racial adversity and structural racism, has been linked to increased risks of cardiovascular disease, heart attacks and chronic health problems in Black groups[15,16,17,18,19]. **Black excellence** peddles incessant goal-striving, the idea of working extra hard and by any means necessary to 'make it', as the way we should be. It is the 'die rich or die trying' mentality, which is fundamentally tyrannical. We cannot work our way out of white supremacy. We cannot excel our way out of racism. The pressure that keeps us striving to do so is racism. Black excellence is a rebranding of **respectability politics**. The idea that emulating white middle class values, presentation and culture can 'uplift the race' and get rid of caricatures of Blackness as intellectually deficient, doomed to eternal poverty and illiteracy. This aspiration to Black exceptionalism fails to consider classist and capitalistic thinking and cannot be separated from racist logic. Emulating the master's politics reifies the master's superiority and their contempt for Blackness.

─── **SUMMARY** ───

1.

The historical load that the Black body carries is almost impossible to escape from and this history gets reproduced at work: It can manifest in the extra scrutiny Black bodies attract from bosses and peers and the difficulties we experience being accepted within white spaces.

2.

Stereotypes, projections and projective identification all colliding can lead to unfair and biased performance appraisals: More significantly they can challenge the boundaries of our minds and lead to us enacting negative expectations.

3.

Control or surveillance measures in the workplace and within white spaces cannot be separated from control and surveillance measures in the broader socio-political context: in the same way we have argued socio-political sovereignty cannot be separated from personal sovereignty.

4.

The lived experience of working while Black is complex and it continues to be, for far too many of us, a story of exclusion, a story of exhaustion and a story of alienation that can lead to distress and racial trauma.

In the next chapter, **BLACK LOVE**, we will consider the impact of racism on intimate and romantic relationships and the ways racism can shape how we love and who we love.

RACE REFLECTIONS

To understand the experience of working while Black it is necessary to connect past and present to recognise relational patterns that continue to lead to exclusion, marginalisation and Othering. This section gives you the opportunity to reflect and develop skills to help resist and navigate the workplace and help protect your body and mind.

What have you found most troubling in this chapter?

You may want to explore your physical responses, images and thoughts that came to you and explore what they might take you back to. Please use the Race Reflections reflective model (p.207) to help you.

....

....

....

....

....

What key obstacles have you faced in your career and what strategies have you built to navigate them?

Assessing the reality of what working while Black has meant can be scary and uncomfortable, but it is not possible to plan resistance and self-care strategies without contemplating the challenge. Please make a list of these challenges.

....

....

....

....

....

Thinking of ourselves outside of work achievements helps build an independent identity so we aren't only dependent on work outcomes for life satisfaction.

Who you are is not determined by others' ability to recognise your abilities. You are much more than your work or job title. What are the things that matter to you? What are your values? What kind of contribution do you want to make to the world?

....

....

....

....

....

We have seen that the same politics at national or geopolitical level shapes how the Black body is treated and how breaches of boundaries occur frequently and threaten our bodily and psychological autonomy and sovereignty.

Take time to consider your boundaries and see whether you do all you can to protect yourself from intrusion at work. What expectations exist where you work that may put you at risk? What stereotypes do you fear confirming? How might you hold on to your sense of identity (including your talents and aptitudes) at work?

....

....

....

....

....

ACTION POINT
STRATEGISE

One of the most helpful actions you can take when it comes to navigating the workplace while Black is to have an overall strategy about how you are going to maximise the chance of you achieving your career goals.

This strategy must consider race-based challenges you are likely to face on your way and tools and resources you can draw from to attempt to overcome them. The point here is not to create a false illusion that what we achieve at work is only within our control; it is not. Rather it is to have a plan, to be prepared psychologically and practically.

Your action point: You have spent some time reflecting on common challenges and on the challenges you have faced – make a list of all the resources you turn to for support. These may include things like:

- Identifying allies (particularly those in positions of seniority) in and outside the workplace and if possible, getting one of them to mentor you.

- Getting to know and considering joining support structures that may exist to protect your rights (e.g. unions, Citizens Advice, Black employee groups).

- Developing a side hustle to increase your options, financial autonomy and confidence.

- Maintaining relationships with colleagues and bosses who have been supportive.

- Seeking others who may share your experience to combat isolation and marginalisation.

Once you have that list, take steps to make sure these support systems are accessible. This will entail ensuring contact and communication is established and maintained so these resources may be ready to use when you need them.

CHAPTER 7

BLACK LOVE

I grew up never seeing a doll that looked like me. When I was a child, Black dolls were unheard of in France. Even today they are still hard to find in mainstream stores. To this date, if I happen to be in a store that sells Black dolls (the darker the better), I find it hard to resist buying them and marvelling at them. Like many French Black people of my generation who are mildly socially conscious and grew up with no Black dolls, before becoming a parent I had fantasies about buying lots of Black dolls for my unborn child. A cousin fulfilled that fantasy. She bought her daughter a Black doll a few years ago for her birthday. She waited anxiously, anticipating her daughter's reaction as she unwrapped the present. Instead of joy, sadness, tears and a temper tantrum followed. 'Why would you buy me an ugly doll?' she cried. Her mother's jaw dropped. She had not seen this coming. There was nothing unusual in the doll's appearance. In fact, you could argue there was nothing remotely Black about it as far as features went if you looked carefully. She even had waist length straight brown hair. But the source of the young child's distress was that she had picked up the notion that lighter was prettier. That Black doll was ugly, and she was inconsolable.

We started *Living While Black* centring love as an antidote to racial trauma. Radical love. The politics of Black love are complex and Black love, arguably like all matters pertaining to Blackness, is a political issue. Historically, Black people have been taught to see each other with disdain and suspicion. To see ourselves as undesirable and unworthy of love and care. These notions can only be fully understood if we situate them within a framework of interlocking systems of oppression: racism, classism and sexism. In this chapter we explore the complexities of Black love, revisit internalised racism and propose tools and strategies to heal our often deeply wounded relationships.

THE CONTEXT OF LOVE

Psychologists Kenneth and Mamie Clark[1] (1947) had already discovered that children favour white dolls about half a century ago. Their famous 'doll tests' experiments, which aimed to document the psychological effects of segregation on African-American children, found that both Black and white children preferred white dolls when given the choice between two identical dolls differing only in terms of skin tone. More worryingly, when asked to explain their choice, children as young as three ascribed negative attributes to Black dolls, such as being mean, being lazy and being ugly. The 253 children who participated in the study were ages 3–7. These children had already learnt that white was right. The Clarks' study contributed to the ending of school segregation in the US as it gave evidence that segregation created feelings of inferiority in Black children and affected their psychological health. Clearly the story of my niece in the mid-2010s, in France, a child who has never known legal segregation, shows the reach of this phenomenon. The research has been replicated inside and outside the US, sometimes with different results but often with the same.

Attractiveness plays a fundamental role in the social allocation of resources that include material resources and power. Research has shown that those deemed attractive tend to do better structurally[2]. They are also more sought after romantically. We cannot talk with honesty about love and loving relationships without speaking about attractiveness. And, who we deem attractive, we treat more favourably. When it comes to criteria for women's attractiveness, constructions of beauty and femininity are intrinsically linked, and such constructions have always been central to systems of domination and marginalisation. It is not coincidental that 'low rank' women (and people more generally) have been socially constructed as less desirable. So, the alleged lack of femininity of disabled women, trans women, poor women, elderly women, and women of colour, especially dark-skinned Black women, continues to be used to dehumanise us. To keep us at the margins of society and justify the violence we experience.

INTERRACIAL LOVE

I want to consider mixed race relationships at this juncture. No doubt many may be tempted to interrogate this decision. The stereotype of the bitter and angry Black woman comes to mind. It is a device often employed when we attempt to explore the impact of white supremacy in romantic relationships. And a device often intended to stop us from investigating social issues that deeply impact our lives[3]. If you are curious about where I stand, in the interest of transparency, I will say this: I have nothing against mixed relationships of any configurations. Attempting to legislate love and physical attraction is the epitome of human futility. Nonetheless, this should not stop us from contextualising such relationships and exploring mixed relationships as a rich site for exploration of both inter and intra group race relations, which can therefore help us understand the complexities of racial trauma and intergenerational wounds[4].

According to the 2011 UK census, 9% of people in a relationship were in an inter-ethnic relationship in England and Wales[5]. This has increased from 7% in 2001. Of note, 'Other Black' (62%) were the second highest (non-mixed/multiple) group most likely to be in an interracial relationship. White Brits (4%) were least likely to be in inter-ethnic relationships, followed by Bangladeshi (7%), Pakistanis (9%) and

Indians (12%). Of all people in inter-ethnic relationships, 40% included someone who was white British. In the US, the picture is strikingly dissimilar[6]. Overall, the most common type of interracial marriage is between white and Hispanic (all races confounded), which account for 38% of all interracial marriages in 2010. White–Asian couples accounted for another 14% of interracial marriages and white–Black couples made up 8%. Across both countries Black men are much more likely to be in mixed relationships than Black women.

The patterns call for some reflection. Why such a discrepancy? Why are mixed relationships not shared equally between the genders in Black groups? One key difference between the UK and US context is the legal history of interracial relationships. Miscegenation or the 'interbreeding' of people considered to be of different racial groups was unlawful for most of US history. It was only legalised in 1967[7]. Various fears underpinned this social taboo, including politics of eugenics and racial purity and fantasised threats to one's nation's health, blood line and security to name a few. Black races constructed as morally, genetically and intellectually inferior needed to be kept away from the white genetic pool in order to protect white supremacy and the social order as evidenced by the 'one drop rule'. The one drop rule is the racial classification principle that dictated that if anyone, no matter what they look like, had a known Black ancestor, that person would automatically be classified as Black[8].

The fear of whiteness being contaminated by Blackness also reflected a deep fear of being outnumbered by Black people in the colonies, where white settlers were long the minority. Policing love has always been policing the boundaries of power. What is more, the possibility that African Americans carry within their consciousness and with more vivacity the sexual horrors carried out on American soil cannot be discounted. Amid miscegenation fantasies, there is ample evidence that rape was a central feature of slavery. A legacy that means today, genetic databases suggest that on average 24% of the African American gene pool can be traced back to

European ancestry. Of course, the rape of slaves and of colonial subjects was a common practice across the Americas including the Caribbean and across colonised Africa, and thus affected the racial composition in the West Indies and to a much lesser extent that in African colonies. Some may argue that this is a history Black Brits can more easily disconnect from because the sexual horrors were not primarily carried out on Britain's soil. This allowed some distancing from that historical violence. Although, if we consider that loving Black–white relationships both in the US and UK disproportionately involve a Black man, perhaps the sexual atrocities carried out on Black women's bodies and the associated trauma also play a part in how Black women relate to white men among other factors. Perhaps there is a taboo that is still alive.

MISOGYNOIR: WHEN RACISM IS GENDERED/ SEXISM IS RACIALISED

The devaluation of Black women's bodies is alive and well. I remember when in May 2011, *Psychology Today* published an article by UK-based evolutionary psychologist Satoshi Kanazawa titled 'Why Are Black Women Less Physically Attractive Than Other Women?'. The article was met with mass outrage[9]. It made several claims including that 'Black women are objectively less physically attractive than other women' yet 'subjectively considered themselves to be far more physically attractive than others.' In the news, we continue to see Black politicians and public figures called ugly, bestialised or compared to animals, and denigrated because of their appearance.

Black people's bodies have long been consumed yet devaluated under the institutions of colonialism and slavery. And, more so, the Black female body. This body was not only viewed as inferior in intelligence, sophistication and as being lower down the chain of evolution, it was also ugly, abnormal, animalistic, hyper-sexual, athletic and masculine. The promotion of white-cis-hetero-patriarchy has been central to the colonial construction of femininity. It places at opposite poles black and white women, purity, grace and beauty arbitrarily accorded to white women and depravity, bestiality and androgyny fixed onto constructions of Black womanhood. This is done to bolster a European aesthetic and thus white womanhood. Nowhere is the arbitrariness of these constructions more observable than when white women and other women of colour receive praise and admiration for features typically devalued in Black women[10]. This tells us three things: First, that beauty is arbitrary at least to a large extent. Second, that the constructed beauty of specific features is very much dependent on who carries them. Finally, beauty is fundamentally linked to power.

In 2000, American feminist theorist and academic Dr Patricia Hill Collins called dominant stereotypes of Black women 'controlling images'[11]. These have been used through times to restrict Black women's freedom, exercise social control, and maintain white capitalist patriarchal interests. Those stereotypes have their origin in Hill Collins' study of African American representation over the ages. They reveal intersections of systems of race, gender and class oppression and their role in both the distribution of material resources, but also in the politics of love, which can illuminate the complexities of fostering Black love within white supremacy. Each of them reflects white supremacy's vested interests in keeping Black women subservient. They include:

The mammy

The stereotype of the mammy is the portrayal of the Black woman as obedient and dedicated to caring for her white master and his family. The mammy is a docile domestic servant, who derives pleasure from completing domestic chores and looking after white children. The mammy image is the social expectation when it comes to Black womanhood. She is the good Black woman. Nurturing, content in servitude and committed to the welfare of white folks, she sacrifices her own needs for the needs of the white family. Hill Collins argues that the mammy trope symbolises the dominant group's fear of Black women's sexuality.

The matriarch

The matriarch is the dominant, aggressive and overbearing Black woman. She is a failed mother. She is a failed wife too. The matriarch 'emasculates' Black men and drives them away. The matriarch is essentially a failed mammy. She works way too hard and away from home, which takes her away from her children, which is seen as neglectful. It is the alleged neglect of Black matriarchs that supposedly leads to poor behaviour, poor educational achievements, crimes in Black communities and the fractures that exist within Black families.

The welfare mother

The welfare mother is characterised by her inability to stop procreating. She has children she cannot afford and is dependent on the state and is therefore the cause of her own poverty. She is to blame for the poverty in African American communities. The welfare mother's unrestrained capacity to produce more Black children speaks of a deep fear of being taken over and outnumbered by Black people. But it also speaks of the presumed lack of morality and responsibility of Black women.

The Jezebel

The final controlling image is the Jezebel, who is all about sexual aggression and 'promiscuity'. She is the forever horny Black woman who exists for the sexual satisfaction of men. This image is deeply linked to slavery's construction of Black women as dangerous temptresses who could lure white men away from saintly Christ-approved sex with white women. The Jezebel stereotype hyper-sexualises Black women and affords them magic sexual powers over men. The stereotype was, of course, handy to justify the sexual abuse, rape and exploitation of Black women by both Black and white men.

What these tropes also lay bare is wishful revisioning of history via projection. They allow Black women to be held responsible for the success or failure of romantic relationships within Black communities. As such, they bear much relevance to Black womanhood over the diaspora. Everyday language to stereotype Black women in Britain, such as: bossy, fierce, controlling, bullish, fiery, lazy, slutty to name but a few, neatly map onto Hill Collins' analysis.

In her hard-hitting essay published in 2013[12], which gave birth to a chapter in *Don't Touch My Hair*[13], Irish historian Emma Dabiri examines the lack of visibility and erasure of Black women in representations of mainstream Black British culture. Such is the erasure that you would be 'forgiven for thinking we are an endangered species', she writes. She notes that Black men and white women dominate representations of love in the British media and the enduring taboo around this social phenomenon. Dabiri also references the controlling images to make sense of the exclusion of Black women in British media. She suggests that this ensures their gendered and racial subordination and sees them facing rejection and denigration from those Black men who aspire to be in relationships with more socially-valued women. Women whose aesthetics are judged to be superior, even in their eyes and those of their peers.

There is no doubt that systemic racism harms Black family structures. In the US in the 1920s, 90% of Black children were born to married parents; it was 80% by the late 1950s and it is about 20% today[14,15]. These numbers portray contemporary difficulties with Black love in the US. Black men are vulnerable to being removed from their communities because of structural injustices and enduring social inequalities[16]. This means that Black women have advanced at a faster rate in education and the job market. This gendered difference in socio-economic positioning can provide further fuel and tension as it echoes historical scripts and trauma around wounded manhood and men's impaired capacity to protect their partners and family in Black groups, which is still an enduring gendered social expectation in **cisgendered heterosexual** (cishet) relationships.

Black women are not exempt from internalising systems of oppression including white patriarchy and classism. It is difficult to imagine that Black men's reduced capacity to offer material protection to Black women and access structures of power would play zero role in how we relate. Still extraordinarily little is known about this reciprocal dynamic and how it leads to the performance of Black love.

Again, in terms of intergenerational context, enslaved Black men were commonly removed and departed from their loved ones and communities[17]. Violated and humiliated in front of their partners and families. They also witnessed their families and partners being brutalised and raped. This context, many believe, has created difficulties in lasting intimate relationships with men or women. Difficulties, on the one hand, that are made worse by disrupted attachments and bonds as we have seen in Chapter 4.

Case study: Alicia

The first time I met Alicia, my jaw almost dropped. She was truly one of the most striking women I had ever laid eyes on. Alicia was a queer Black woman in her early twenties, tall, dark and statuesque with perfectly drawn African features. She came to see me because she was feeling low and had a history of depression. She fought tears throughout most of our first session, self-conscious it seemed about being vulnerable in front of the total stranger I still was. She complained about not liking herself very much. She had a history of sexually abusive relationships and was a serial dater of white people, mainly men. She struggled to get on romantically with Black people. She said she simply did not get their attention. As I observed her, almost unable to maintain eye contact with me, it was difficult to reconcile how she viewed herself with who I saw sitting in the chair in front of me. But this was not a

> *performance and it became obvious very quickly that this dysmorphic relationship Alicia had with her body was racialised. She hated her nose. She hated her lips. She was not fond of her skin. She informed me she was the darkest person in her family. She repeated this a few times. People would stare at her, she would say to me, tearing up. She thought they stared because she was ugly or weird. And that something must be wrong with her. It took us almost two years for Alicia to start changing her relationship with her body, which coincided with her stopping dating white people exclusively.*

There is a lot that has historical resonance when considering Alicia's story. We see in it a troubled relationship with her body and with her sexuality. We see too a troubled relationship with her colour and racialised features. There are also important themes of abuse and invisibility. Alicia sought multiple sexual partners who were white, but she was aware there was something troubling in her relationship with white people. Alicia was dependent on their sexual attention to maintain the little self-esteem she had, yet every time she was ill-treated, her self-love plummeted. Still the attraction to whiteness kept her in a vicious cycle of dependency.

Fanon perfectly articulated the desire for white sexual partners as the desire for whiteness[18]. For women, this desire cannot be separated from the need for material security and access to structures of power. Acceptance into high society or structures of power becomes a metaphor for being accepted into whiteness regardless of the psychological costs and loss of dignity. The complexity and poignancy of these words is that seeking white partners is a form of self-harm for Fanon, who in fact questions whether love across the racial divide is attainable with Black inferiority and white superiority as constant. Fanon suggests that in this context authentic love is virtually impossible as this positioning towards whiteness is born out of a need to defend ourselves against feelings of insignificance and a disowned need for white approval. Such impulses are therefore a call to turn white.

Racial whitening was an ideology common in South America and part of the Caribbean that attempted to bring Black people up the class hierarchy[19]. Racial whitening was therefore practised to advance Black people culturally and genetically with support from scientific racism. We see echoes of internalised whiteness in Alicia's attempt to seek a sense of self-worth and validation from the white gaze regardless of how abusive. This reproduces a cycle of relational self-harm that is bolstered by her self-hatred. But similarly, we may be curious about the treatment she has experienced at the hands of Black people. Once aware of the historical issues we have covered, we can better resist the repetition of history.

LOVE AT THE INTERSECTIONS

Finding love and sustaining love amid racism is not the complete story. We have seen how racism, sexism and classism bear strong influence on Black love. Many of us must also deal with homophobia, ableism and other axes of oppression, their intersections, and the additional challenges they bring to already complex terrain. Multiple marginalised identities can be highly stigmatised within Black communities[20]. Part of this stigma is a residue of the intergenerational context. For example, many countries in Africa still have homophobic laws put into effect by European colonisers[21]. Black immigrants would have come from cultures or countries where homosexuality is simply socially unacceptable and, in some places, carries the risk of state-sanctioned death. In the Caribbean, the taboo of homosexuality, has, in part, been linked to the rape or torture of male slaves[22]. Across the diaspora the legacy of medical racism can manifest in disabled people bringing 'shame' onto the 'Black race' and evidence of our inhumanity.

Much of the stigma here is likely related to the politics of respectability and our collective internalisation of inferiority. It is not a surprise that those located at the intersections of axes of oppression will have qualitatively different experiences of Black love and intimacy. Many of us experience a sense of being doubly or triply unlovable, doubly or triply excluded from intimacy. These multi-layered experiences of Otherness heighten experiences of isolation, which can compound unsafeness and make it hard to trust in relationships. In the case of queer love for example, for many in our community it is not safe to live one's love openly and this means feeling unsafe and unwelcome because of queer/homo/bi/transphobia and finding no refuge within white society including mainstream LGBTQIA+ spaces because of anti-Blackness. All while losing ties to one's heritage and cultural home and, with that, support networks and traditions which many depend on for wellbeing, security and belonging.

As a result, LGBTQIA+ Black people are at high risk of psychological distress, self-harm and suicide and many continue to be at significant risk of harm[23]. In terms of love, the lack of social support can translate into the pressure to stay in relationships that may be abusive or unfulfilling due to fear of being alone and losing another source of support, a tangible lived reality. Furthermore, much of what we know about functioning in relationships we learn from observing relationships around us, particularly that of our parents and images in the media. There are additional challenges for our queer siblings. The lack of representation of queer Black love further limits access to appropriate role models when it comes to navigating multiple traumas and maintaining loving relationships.

Still, there are reasons to be hopeful. Objection to narrow, heteronormative, white-dominated love is mounting across the globe. Stories, images and representations of love we have been excluded from are becoming accessible. Allowing those who have had to live their love in the shadows for too long to take space with pride. There is a new generation engaged in addressing intergenerational trauma and seeking help. Therapy, for example, appears to be losing its taboo. We are talking more and are increasingly aware of what we have inherited and what we're choosing to leave behind.

Younger generations are challenging what love means and what relationships should look like, contesting Eurocentric notions of love.

In the UK, a coalition of public figures such as model Jourdan Dunn, presenter Clara Amfo, Team GB boxer Nicola Adams, journalist Yomi Adegoke and spoken-word artist George the Poet have come together to launch a campaign to make Black Love more visible and inclusive. #MyLoveIs-BlackLove aims to showcase Black love in its multitude and to be more representative of what Black love looks like in Britain today. Finally, Busy Being Black, a compendium of queer Black voices, is gaining prominence. It showcases an oral history project and a podcast centring 'those who have learnt – and are learning – to thrive at the intersections of their identities'. Busy Being Black, like so many coalitions of black queer love, is all about challenging narrow, heteronormative, white-dominated love. And so, stories, images and representations of love we have been deprived of are becoming accessible, if not centre stage. The future of Black love is looking bright and rainbow.

SUMMARY

1.

There are many challenges associated with Black love: they are better understood by locating them within a historical and the intergenerational context.

2.

Constructions of beauty and attractiveness, which play a fundamental role in the social allocation of resources and power and femininity, have traditionally excluded the Black female body.

3.

Interlocking systems of oppression make seeing each other as we are an ongoing challenge.

4.

Enduring social inequality and experience of racism that are mediated by gendered stereotypes and cis-gendered heterosexual norms put stress and strain on our intimate relationships: particularly for those whose Blackness meets queerness.

In the next and final chapter, **BLACK RESISTANCE**, we contextualise our long history of defiance and insurgency and look at tools that can help us thrive and resist white supremacy.

RACE REFLECTIONS

Our intimate and romantic relationships are not exempt from the influence of racism and racial trauma. Given how vital our close bonds are in terms of support, connection and welfare it is vitally important that we invest as much as we can to attempt to heal the wounds of racial trauma. This section gives you the opportunity to reflect on love and intimacy.

What have you found most troubling in this chapter?

You may want to explore your bodily responses, images and thoughts that came to you and explore what they might take you back to. Please use the Race Reflections reflective model (p.207) to help you.

....

....

....

....

....

Maintaining love for one another, amid structural racism, can be a minefield, but that Black love is fundamental to our wellness and resistance.

What are the key challenges faced in your romantic relationships and what strategies have you built to overcome them? Knowing what you now know, what would you do differently?

....

....

....

....

....

Our earlier relationships and romantic role models can affect how we relate to partners.

Watching your parents and those around you, who do you want to carry with you and who do you want to leave behind moving forward? Who are your role models when it comes to love/Black love? Take time to consider racism, sexism and other axes of oppression.

....

....

....

....

....

Images and gendered and/or racialised stereotypes deeply affect how we see and treat one another romantically, making it challenging to see ourselves for who we are. Re-evaluate any problematic notions centring love and compassion.

Take time to consider what racism has taught you about people of different genders that might be negatively impacting your intimate relationship(s), and how you might have in the past reacted as a result.

....

....

....

....

....

I sometimes say that showing love loudly and deliberately is necessary to counterbalance the covert and overt hatred that Blackness attracts. Think about it: we live in a world where we are much more likely to see Black bodies brutalised or policed in public than we are to see them being loved unapologetically at school gates, on the streets or on our screens. Remedying this unbalance is a political act. But it is likely also a public health matter. We need to show one another unconditional love, and to do so without restraint or reservations, to reclaim our humanity.

Your action point: You are therefore invited to make a love pledge. To show love consciously and deliberately to Black people, to leave those who matter to you in no doubt about your love for them. Think about how you show love to those close to you and to those around you. Ask those you are intimate with how you can love them better and tell them how they can help you feel loved, then commit to loving one another better.

CHAPTER 8

BLACK RESISTANCE

Some of my earliest memories in mental health wards have stayed with me. I cherish them. They have truly shaped me as a psychologist. One such experience happened early in my psychology journey, about 15 years ago in London. A psychologist, who was a woman of colour, complained to me about Black patients she had been allocated to work with. This was as part of a specific service available to Black people. Frustrated, she moaned: 'it's impossible to work with these patients, they're stuck on racism,' then casually walked away, angry, leaving me puzzled. It took several years for me to even come close to grasping the racism contained within this simple statement and the history it laid bare. Revisiting this experience now triggers anger in me. It would be impossible to grasp the violence of this exchange without looking once more at history. In this chapter we consider Black resistance. We have covered a lot of ground in *Living While Black* and thought a lot about living and surviving. It is important we remember that the only reason we are here is because of our history of resistance. Our history of wanting better. Our history of continuing to believe that despite all odds, freedom is possible.

In this chapter we consider what Black resistance might look like today and some of the tools we may use not only to live but to thrive while Black.

THE PATHOLOGISATION OF BLACK RESISTANCE

Drapetomania and Rascality

Drapetomania was believed to be an inheritable but preventable 'mental illness' that caused enslaved Africans to run away and flee captivity, often repeatedly and always against their best interests. Their best interests, of course, being dutifully serving their white master – bending the knee. Rascality, scientifically known as Dysesthesia Aethiopica, on the other hand, was a disease of the mind characterised by laziness, defiance, lack of work ethics and mischievous behaviour. This mischief was clear. It was always related to indifference and disregard or to the sabotaging of the interests of the master. Contrary to Drapetomania, Rascality could helpfully be recognised by clear physical symptoms that were visible. They could appear as marks and lesions on the back of the sufferer, for example, showcasing not only their insensitive skin but also their diseased mind. Such mental illnesses were so serious and communicable that they led to countless rebellions including the liberation of Haiti. Thus, they instilled fear in the hearts of white slave owners.

This historical context reminds us that mental health disciplines, psychiatry and medicine have long histories of racism[1]. But more than that, it tells us something of critical significance about the role that the 'sciences of the mind' have played in the production and reproduction of the dominant values of society and how deeply invested in the maintenance of the racialised social order they have been. We can also see that the practice of silencing Black people, their social realities however violent, however unjust, however torturous, however traumatic, has been normative and that those seeking to challenge or change unequal structures have always been at risk of pathologisation and violence within health systems.

Even though Black people have been pathologised for resisting oppression, we have never been passive recipients of racist violence. As we will explore, there is a long-documented history of Black resistance dating as far back as the earliest encounter on the African coastline. By resistance we simply mean the process of opposing racism and race-based domination and working towards liberation. We resisted even when it meant inevitable death. It is within that struggle for resistance that we have continued to assert our humanity and right to exist free from racism. Resistance has also allowed us to keep our sanity even though it has made those set on refusing to see us as humans, see us as insane.

FORMS OF RESISTANCE

Resistance has taken several forms. During the middle passage, uprisings and suicides were common. On plantations, resistance meant damaging the master's property or machinery or running away despite the obvious risks. Clearly, Drapetomania was contagious. It is that spirit of resistance that has ensured the survival of many of the cultural practices we can easily recognise across the diaspora. The survival of African customs, religious beliefs, names and music were fundamental ways to resist the complete erasure of one's heritage and indoctrination into whiteness. This resistance has, of course, always attracted severe sanction, violence or pathologisation.

Nowhere is this truer than within the mental health system. My early experience on the ward in London may on the surface look quite different to the process by which Black people in southern plantations were diagnosed with Drapetomania. Different until we consider the group who exasperated the psychologist, for being 'stuck on racism', is part of a group of service users who have received some of the most adverse mental health 'care' imaginable, as per Chapter 2. Many had spoken about police officers sitting on their back during arrests or mental health staff restraining them to the point of broken bones. All had been deprived of their liberties. The violence they attempted to articulate and to process with someone whose job it is to primarily listen was disturbing too. Despite this, these vulnerable patients clearly in need of support for racial trauma and support in their resistance were, and continue to be, failed.

Today, subtler ways of pathologising resistance can be found in and outside the mental health system. It is this pathologisation that betrays the assumption that there is nothing worth protesting about or worth changing in the unjust social order. And/or that psychological maturity is assessed by our capacity to accept and adapt to racial injustice – hence why we should not name racism and certainly not seek to resist it. And why that resistance is pathological.

Psychological resistance

One of the most common dilemmas we must face and that I encounter clinically is whether to resist or accept racism. Sometimes people conclude that they must choose their battles because constantly fighting against racism can be hazardous when the stuff is everywhere. There certainly is much truth to this. Although, in fact, once more there are various ways to resist. I often remind people who come to see me and are anxious that they are not doing resistance right that we are all trying to figure out how to navigate racism. There is no magic formula. If there was, it would have been discovered by now. Racism is an animal that continually adapts and evolves and twists and turns. During such gymnastics, having a large repertoire of behavioural and psychological resistance strategies is necessary.

Yet, it is true too that some of us may think racism is just a part of life, and they may say they are scared to speak out. Let us address these issues in turn.

Researchers have examined coping mechanisms and responses to racism and their impact on trauma symptoms. In this kind of research, passive coping mechanisms such as accepting that there is nothing we can do about racism and active coping mechanisms (for example: organising) are usually compared. Individuals who show an acceptance of race discrimination and who, for instance, tend to keep racism to themselves tend to report significantly higher levels of distress or trauma 'symptoms'[2] than those who name their experiences and challenge them[3, 4].

It is also true that our coping and resistance strategies often expose us to more racism. Speaking up or instigating formal complaints has been linked to further racism through retaliation from institutions or from those in a position of power increasing risks of racial trauma[5]. Nonetheless more must be said about fear. White terror has long been used to terrorise those who sought to engage in resistance. There is a long history of torture, sadistic punishment and grotesque murder of those who resisted racial oppression[7]. The infliction of torture and pain to dominate or control and thus protect white economic interests has reigned. Over time, there is little doubt that violence has left collective scars in the form of intergenerational fears of resistance within families. The passing down of acceptance and silence to survive.

Silence as resistance

'The function, the profoundly serious function, of racism is distraction. It keeps you from doing your work. It keeps you explaining, repeatedly, your reason for being. Somebody says you have no language, and you spend twenty years proving that you do. Somebody says your head is not shaped properly so you have scientists working on the fact that it is. Somebody says you have no art, so you dredge that up. Somebody says you have no kingdoms, so you dredge that up. None of this is necessary. There will always be one more thing' – Toni Morrison[6].

We have repeatedly said in this book that silence is often a consequence of trauma[9]. There is nonetheless one area where silence may be more adaptive. Silence as refusal to engage. Silence here is a form of psychological boundary and can be a powerful way to refuse to centre whiteness and to debate our humanity.

This is the reason why I advocate non-engagement with white people who dispute matters related to white privilege, oppression and racism. Let them be. Often, this means letting them feel intellectually superior and comfortable in their uncritical notions of objectivity. Learning to unhook ourselves from this sadistic interaction is central to us keeping sufficient energy to focus on our liberation. The emotional labour of engaging in such debate is not worth it. And we need to recognise that there are simply too many more important things to do with our time and energy. Life is short. Why waste another single moment of it entertaining bigotry dressed as reason. Toni Morrison said this more eloquently than any of us ever could: 'the function of racism is distraction.' We cannot reason our way out of racism.

Engaging in debates is a waste of time. I repeat: engaging in debates is a waste of time. But more than a waste of time, it is psychologically taxing. Meaningful dialogue requires reciprocity, the willingness to treat the Other as an equal and to trust their experience. This is what engaging in good faith entails. White supremacy does not seek to engage in good faith – it seeks to maintain supremacy. It will twist, turn, and forever shift to maintain its superiority as you make yourself ill trying to prove you are being harmed. None of that is necessary. Making our existence and our lived reality subject to agreement, debate or approval is maintaining power relations by making the existence of racism dependent on the approval or understanding of those who enact racism, those whose very sense of self depends on the erasure of the violence they enact. In this context, silence IS resistance.

In this line of thought, author and journalist Reni Eddo-Lodge's[7] *Why I'm No Longer Talking to White People About Race* made the point perfectly. She writes:

'I'm no longer engaging with white people on the topic of race. Not all white people, just the clear majority who refuse to accept the existence of structural racism and its symptoms. I can no longer engage with the gulf of an emotional disconnect that white people display when a person of colour articulates their experience. You can see their eyes shut down and harden. It is as if treacle is poured into their ears, blocking up their ear canals. It is like they can no longer hear us.'

Connecting as resistance

One of the reasons why racism inflicts trauma is because it forces us to disconnect. This disconnection is amplified in contexts of exclusion and marginalisation. This cultural homelessness that so many of us must learn to be at home with is constantly triggered by everyday microaggressions and covert Othering messages. It is within this sense of homelessness that so much intergenerational trauma resonates and that is carried through, beyond individualised coping and resistance strategies. There must therefore be community-level healing that nurtures the soul and strengthens our bonds. Racism causes us to disconnect at multiple levels. Disconnect from earth, soil and our environment as adults by avoiding parks and places of greenery for fear of being reported to the police and seen as trespassers. Or when we simply live way too far from them due to environmental or structural racism.

We disconnect from our heritage as we learn to internalise shame about the land, the customs of our forebears and our histories. We disconnect from our minds and bodies because it is near impossible to feel at home within ourselves when we are constantly gaslighted and taught to distrust our embodied realities. And finally, we disconnect from each other, too, as many of us come to be seduced by the thought of sitting at the master's table and re-enacting exclusion and gatekeeping through that scarcity mentality that helps to ensure those who look like us are barred from structures few of us manage to access.

What does more harm to us than these multiple level disconnections? Our ancestral heritage recognises the importance of connection. Resistance must therefore focus on connecting. Connection with our body, mind, community, history and the environment. African-centred conceptualisations of wellness are based on a symbiotic relationship with those and the world around us including with nature, earth, soil and our ancestors. It is that mutual relationship that exists between living and non-living entities that ensures harmony and continuation of the past into the present. From this non-Western perspective, connecting with the land connects us to memories, but also to community and history. It is for this reason that I often suggest to those who return to their ancestral land if they can to connect with soil and, bring some soil back with them.

Case study: Music as resistance

Marie is a Congolese woman seeking asylum in the UK. She is beautiful and in her early thirties. She has experienced and witnessed some of the ugliest violence humans are capable of inflicting on one another. She was tortured, held captive and raped during war. Marie had seen her son mutilated to death. She and I crossed paths in a detention centre in the UK – she hardly spoke English or French. I could hardly speak Lingala. Still, she returned to me again and again. Without appointments. She was battling repeated attempts from the government to deport her, the shameless racism of the hostile environment. A monster of a different kind but a monster, nonetheless. When Marie dropped in, she would look for me and sit close to me, often in silence. One evening toward the end of the working day, she came in and started sobbing uncontrollably. Possibly the most sorrowful tears I have borne witness to. She was back. She was not with me although her body was in the room. I imagined she was reliving massacres. Scenes of war and unspeakable violence. Blood scenes. Scenes of horrors and of loss. It turned out it was the anniversary of the bloody murder of her young son. I sat by her in silence. For perhaps 30 minutes. But I was losing her. She was going deeper and deeper into sorrow. What word of comfort could I even think of giving this horribly traumatised woman who was mourning so painfully the death of her son? How could I reconnect her to the world of the living? Hold her without holding her? And tell her that life was still worth living in the midst of the anti-Black detention she found herself in. Captive, once more, which was compounding her trauma. I stood up, I went to my computer and searched YouTube. I looked for a few Congolese songs and played them. I watched her instantly stand up and start dancing. I joined her. And little by little I could see her rejoining me. Her eyes were alive again. She had returned into the room. Music had brought her back from the dead. And connected us to life.

Engaging with African music took us to a different realm of communication. My intervention with Marie was unusual and intuitive, but our shared Congolese ancestry probably meant I understood perhaps unconsciously the centrality of dancing and music culturally. Current psychological models have not engaged with the worldview and cultural beliefs and values of people of African descent. In fact, it continues to inferiorise them. What is more, the over-focus on the mind and the cognitive has historically marginalised the body. This is at odds with much research that shows the importance of body work and movement in healing trauma. Integrating traditional healing practices into psychotherapy with African and Caribbean clients may address some of the mental health concerns of Black groups.

There are a few noted exceptions related to the exclusion of the body within therapeutic space. **Dance Movement Psychotherapy** (DMP) is one. In DMP therapists and clients use body movement and dance to foster the integration and processing of various parts of the self.[8]

DMP is consistent with African and Caribbean healing traditions as an approach. Further more, the American therapy

Association now recommends harnessing the power of African Caribbean dance healing systems to process trauma and work with damages done by systems of oppression. According to DMP therapist, Maria 'Mara' Rivera, that approach, dance and movement can allow us to reclaim various kinds of powers:

1. **The self-body power**

   The self-body power is about dancing with intention. The intention is to activate healing energy, free intuition, and trust internal resources to do the reparative work. It enables the body to occupy itself.

2. **Collective power**

   Dance has the power to create community connection via the communal spaces it creates. The collective power comes from these spaces, acting as safe container and as a community holding environment for a collective expression, voice and sharing. Traditionally fostering intergenerational connection and the passing on of healing, culture and folklore.

3. **Socio-political power**

   Dancing and power cannot be separated in Black history. It was through dancing that enslaved Africans connected to the spiritual and found the strength to survive and courage to fight for their freedom. Today dancing and music continue to be central to struggles against oppression and injustice and the reclaiming of power.

4. **Spiritual power**

   African and Caribbean dancing has fed our soul since time immemorial. The energy it generates has the potential to connect us to the forces of the universe, to the forces of life, which may lead to a subjective sense of oneness and spiritual alignment.

Resisting hierarchies of Blackness

Hierarchies of Blackness have historically been related to proximity to the master or proximity to whiteness and have therefore relied on colourism. Colourism is the preferential treatment of lighter-skinned people over dark-skinned ones. Historically, children of Black slaves fathered by white masters often gained privileges based on their lighter skin shade, selected to work in the master's house while Blacks of darker hues were routinely sent to the fields where labour was more intensive and treacherous. In the African colonies similar systems were created by colonial powers. In Rwanda for example, colonial administrators exacerbated divisions by only allowing Tutsis, presumed to be light-skinned, to attain higher education and hold positions of power over the dark-skinned Hutus, fueling tensions that significantly contributed to the genocide.

Colourism has enabled Black people to further their education and other life opportunities and has encouraged darker-skinned people to devalue their skin colour or seek to lighten it.[9,10] Over time, class and status distinctions between lighter- and darker-skinned were created in the Americas, Caribbean and Africa, with distinction in skin tone mapping directly onto socio-economic, cultural and political power and privileges. This is what is commonly referred to as Pigmentocracy[11].

Pigmentocracy reproduces white supremacy. Another facet of proximity to whiteness is the hierarchisation of Black lives based on geopolitical location or more accurately, proximity to Africa. The trend across African descendants is to still view Black people in continental Africa as less sophisticated and more 'primitive', in line with colonial fantasies. This leads many people across the diaspora to disown ancestral ties, Africanness and to a tendency to see the plight of siblings in Africa as distinct or separate from our experience in Europe or in the US. This is a fallacy.

But white supremacy starts with the most expendable lives, which tend to be in the Global South. But it does not stop there. It never has. And so the impunity that protects European states from accountability when it comes to the drowning of Black lives in the Mediterranean – Black lives attempting to seek safety and security from conflicts often orchestrated to sustain neo-colonial interests – creates the type of extreme trauma we saw in Marie. It is the same impunity that ensures that state-sanctioned violence and brutality against Black bodies is allowed to go unpunished in Britain, in the US and in other parts of the West. And the disregard for Black African lives simply feeds into the contempt towards Black bodies everywhere on the planet.

Colonialism and capitalist exploitation of Africa has resulted in catastrophic, irrevocable damage to our planet and led to the global inequalities that threaten peace and harmony in the world. So-called discussions about 'development' therefore fit within a wider discussion about environmental damage, racial injustice and racial trauma. Marie's trauma reminds us of the trauma of millions located in or fleeing exploited nations and bears close resemblance to the colonial violence that marked the consciousness, and unconsciousness, of such nations. It is no coincidence, for example, that countries with the most brutal colonial histories continue to suffer the most brutal conflicts today. That wherever rape and sexual abuse were used as mass weapons of colonial subjugation, where mutilation and unspeakable torture were normalised, we continue to see them today used as weapons of war. Remember, nations can suffer trauma too. And again, trauma tends to lead to repetition.

When we see our fates and suffering as interconnected, we resist 'divide and rule' and hierarchies of Blackness that fundamentally reproduce white supremacy. Reclaiming the most devalued, the most disenfranchised, the darkest and poorest among us is a powerful demonstration of self-love. It is resisting whiteness and all deriving hierarchies.

Beauty as resistance

In *And Still I Rise*[12] Maya Angelou powerfully articulates her capacity to connect with her beauty and her erotic power.

Qualities that, despite violent erasure attempts, remain. She evokes the misogyny and racism, contemporarily and historically, that she and generations of Black women before her have endured. Yet her poem is one of triumph, one of survival. Not only have we survived, we are thriving and gaining strength, beauty and power not despite but because of racial adversity. Though this may challenge common wisdom around the hierarchisation and posited pyramids of human needs, there is a long history of marginalised people seeking affirmation through beauty. Black artists and others, for example, have used fashion and style as means to resist oppression for centuries. From the slaves who took pride in their appearance and beauty by dressing in their Sunday best, to the dandies of the Harlem Renaissance and the sapeurs of the Congo[13,14].

These efforts were never simply about vanity, narcissism or emulating the master. They have always been about politics, about challenging colonial narratives about self-love and self-definition. We know that connection with beauty during war has been a way to assert one's humanity. An activist recounted the story of such a woman who had spoken about how important it was for her to die beautiful and that if she was to be killed by a sniper, she wanted her killer to know that he was putting a beautiful woman to death. Few domains exist where marginalised women can feel valued and take control of how they are represented. The subordination of our needs is socially expected and as part of that, self-negation and self-hatred are viewed as standard. Wearing lipstick during the war had become a way for some to assert their humanity.

bell hooks teaches us that self-love is dangerous and threatening in a white supremacist culture. She says it is a 'serious breach in the fabric of the social order'[15]. Reclaiming beauty. Ours. And that exists in the world, through art and through nature. Doing so has always been central to liberation[16]. It buffers the impact of racial injustices. At its most fundamental, caring about the way we look is caring about our body and by extension, our life. It is rejecting notions of inferiority and inadequacy. It is proclaiming: I believe I am entitled to love and thus, to justice and equality. It is quietly saying I am a human being. Like you. Perhaps, this is what so many have a hard time accepting.

Black mediocrity, Black liberation?

It is hard to write about self-care in the middle of global anti-Black warfare. But there is a war too that is happening inside of us. Many of us try to manage it by overachieving. As I write, the idea that for us to be accepted as human we must become superhuman, is still a thing. We must be the next Muhammad Ali of our field. Mediocrity is not an option, it is forbidden to us, therefore being mediocre is not something we dare to allow ourselves to be. Society tells us that to deserve to live, we must have some rare and incredible talent. In art, in sport, in science. In any field, if we are exceptional enough, then people might forgive and forget our Blackness. We might transcend our race, they say. An expression that filled Ali's obituaries, by the way. His greatest achievement was this, it appears. Forget his radical politics. His boxing excellence. Or his sense of justice and ethics. He made white people forget his race. Not when they sent him to jail, mind you. Still, we hear, he made white people connect with him, so many of them tell us, despite his Blackness.

Black excellence is linked to this idea of transcendence[17]. Fundamentally it is the idea that exceptional achievements by Black people, often despite racial adversity, elevate Blackness and counter racist stereotypes about us. Black excellence is of course exclusionary and arguably reproduces materialistic takes on what success look like. It fundamentally centres whiteness as the kid to impress. The internalisation of racism can often mean that we are raised and socialised to prove that we are good enough to be recognised and seen. This posturing fuels the belief that any 'failure' or mediocrity might confirm racial stereotypes or bring shame onto our family or our community[18]. It also shows little consideration to the impact on our health, physical and mental. I find myself remembering conversations I had with a teacher who had been promoted to deputy head in her school and started working 80 hours a week, every week until she became so unwell, she had to be hospitalised. Or again the Black taxi driver who worked at nights and went to university during the day. He suffered the same fate. Both became psychiatric patients. Arguably lucky to be alive.

I have heard of others who did not survive the pressure of Black excellence. When thinking about Black excellence, we must think about how it may be an act of compensation for structural racism but also an act of compensation for shame. Black excellence, insidiously, by parading achievements by Black people, to prove our competence, our capability and ultimately our humanity, reproduces white supremacy and Black shame. The shame we are talking about here comes about as a result of trying to fit into white society, which consistently tells us implicitly or explicitly that we are inferior, threatening or otherwise dysfunctional and that we must assimilate into whiteness, to be human; alienating us from parts of ourselves that many of us then come to despise[19,20]. In other words, race-related shame is a by-product of power structures and of racialised social hierarchies. The shame is linked to survival so it may exist even when we may not have consciously bought into our own inferiority. The awareness that we must 'play the game' to survive may bring it up. It is thus a shame that may also be triggered by the contemplation of our complicity. Thankfully, this is something all of us can become aware of and reduce.

Black pride

When your dignity is repeatedly hit and you witness or experience humiliation and indignity, your sense of pride can fundamentally shift. Although pride is the antidote to shame, it requires work. It is difficult to feel pride when you are not represented, when the history that is sold to the world positions you as inferior. When the harm that was done to you and your ancestors under the guise of 'civilisation' continues to be presented as virtuous. All Black movements for liberation have centred the need for Black pride again, as an act of active defiance. Black pride in this context is a response to white supremacist cultures and ideologies of devaluation, denigration and Othering. It seeks to encourage us to celebrate our heritage, our features and history. It seeks to make us feel good about being Black.

Racism assaults our self-esteem, pride helps maintains it[21]. This is important as research shows self-esteem may help buffer racist experiences and racial trauma. More frequent experiences of racism are associated with lower self-esteem. And higher levels of self-esteem are associated with lower levels of racial trauma. Clearly as Black people, our sense of self-esteem is also connected to our racial identity and thus to race. Racial identity concerns a person's self-categorisation and attachment to both their racial group and their relationship with whiteness. And again, research shows that those whose racial identity centres on conformity to whiteness, on devaluing attitudes towards Blackness and on disconnection or dissonance from their Blackness, are also more psychologically vulnerable within white supremacy.

Acculturation offers us another framework to look at our relation to our racial identity. Broadly speaking, as applied to individuals, acculturation refers to changes that take place as a result of contact between two different cultural groups[22]. Acculturation is most often studied in individuals living in countries or regions other than where they were born, thus among immigrants, refugees, asylum seekers and sojourners. And while it goes without saying that Blackness in the context of Britain or Europe does not imply migration, a large proportion of Black people in the UK or in Europe either have parents or grandparents who were migrants. However, in the US, as we have previously discussed, the foreign-born population is growing. Given the large cultural differences that exists between mainstream white America and African American values, worldview and culture, we may argue that a similar process may need to happen for Black Americans to connect with racial identity development (see Chapter 1). As such the framework is still helpful to think about identity. Acculturation considers migrants' responses to migration and the shifts that occur to their racial and cultural identity because of migration. The model is based on two axes of culture acquisition, which is about how we manage the 'new culture' and heritage retention.

These two dimensions intersect to create four possible acculturation styles:

- Assimilation: when we adopt the dominant culture and discard the culture of our heritage.
- Separation: when we reject the dominant culture and retain the heritage culture.
- Integration: when we both adopt the dominant culture and retain the heritage culture.
- Marginalisation: rejection of both the heritage and culture of our heritage.

There is now substantial evidence that suggests that discarding our culture of origin, or heritage, increases the likelihood of a whole host of negative physical and mental health consequences. Generally, those who manage to maintain some contact with their heritage fare much better than those who do not. It is clear then that maintaining Black pride is more than a political imperative – it must be central to our self-care.

Resistance through spirituality

Spirituality does not have to be tied to any religion although for many of us, religion allows us to connect with the spiritual. Religion and Blackness have a complex relationship. Both Islam and Christianity were imposed on our ancestors. The imperative to forgive has historically been weaponised as illustrated by the words of former Kenyan Prime Minister, Jomo Kenyatta: 'When the Missionaries arrived, the Africans had the land and the Missionaries had the Bible. They taught how to pray with our eyes closed. When we opened them, they had the land, and we had the Bible'[23]. Christianity's love and mercy messages were sold to our ancestors during the arduous Middle Passage, on torturous plantations and on native and African shores upon colonial encounters between white and Black bodies.

There is absolutely no doubt that a version of Christianity was instrumental in progressing imperial and colonial agendas. White agendas. Christianity was used to justify enslavement. To pacify distraught and furious displaced and tortured bodies and souls by offering them the promise of eternal life. It promulgated a vision of a white god as the image of the white colonial master, and it forever traded forgiveness for mass atrocities and inescapable racial violence. Yet enslaved people did use religion to resist and to survive slavery and to reclaim their humanity. Further, African traditions were combined with Christianity, allowing for a new collective identity and pride to be born[24].

Today young Black people are shying away from and leaving organised religious institutions, to connect with African and nature-centred spirituality[25, 26]. Reverence for spirits and the ancestors through the practice of Vodou, Santería, Candomblé or other variations of Yoruba religious traditions is becoming a way to reconnect to one's ancestry while integrating African religious traditions.

Mainstream mental health services are becoming more open to the integration of spiritual practices within mental health care. In the UK, the Royal College of Psychiatrists reported that patients who engage in spiritual practice of some kind gained:

- better self-control, self-esteem, and an increase in confidence.

- faster and easier recovery (often through healthy grieving of losses and through recognising their strengths).
- better relationships with themselves, others and with God/creation/nature.
- a new sense of hope and peace of mind. This has enabled them to accept and live with continuing problems or to make changes where possible[27].

There is therefore a strong case to re-discover or discover some form of spiritual practice to heal from racial trauma.

BLACK JOY

The late Toni Morrison wrote about the mystery of the tree-shaped scar, the beautiful scar left on the back of whipped slaves that eerily reassembles a tree[6]. It is, for me, a visual representation of her work and life mission. A reminder of the importance of finding joy and beauty within ourselves and within this brutal world. Beauty and joy amid the dehumanising and violent reality of white supremacy. Joy amid pain. Powerful aspirations in their simplicity. Powerful also in their humanity. Something that reminds me of the genius of Morrison. Her mastery of the art of making the complex and sophisticated not only accessible but so viscerally beautiful. We struggle in 'our' culture to celebrate and to mourn at the same time but Living While Black is recurrently having to experience anger and pain. The tree-shaped scar is a powerful reminder that beauty can be found in the ugliest of circumstances. And that life can co-exist with death, beauty with pain and growth can take place in the midst of suffering.

Many come to see me because they struggle with finding joy. Finding joy in intimate relationships. Finding joy in connection. Finding joy in sex. Finding joy just existing in the world, while Black. When you cannot find joy for long enough, despair can come knocking and it is easy to let it in. As we have seen in Chapter 2, rates of mental health problems and psychological distress are the highest within Black groups. And again, psychological distress is the antithesis of joy. There are less obvious reasons why many struggle with experiencing joy. We may stop ourselves from experiencing happiness or engage in self-destructiveness out of loyalty for those who have suffered or indeed been destroyed. We may feel compelled to experience feelings that were too dangerous to express or experience by those who came before us. Mourning on their behalf. We may stop ourselves from experiencing joy out of fear that we may be punished or that something terrible may be on its way. We may stop ourselves from connecting with joy because we feel, consciously or otherwise, that we simply do not serve joy. Practising joy must be strategic, and it must be deliberate and like self-care more generally cannot be decontextualised. The ability to create and hold spaces for our joy as individuals and as a group of people is an ongoing struggle. But experiencing joy, even if moments of it, is revolutionary. Joy is a spiritual practice. It connects us to beauty, to wonder, to grace, to pleasure. It is thus an emotion that connects us to life, to the universe and to ourselves and each other. Black joy disturbs whiteness because it is humanising and because it is humanising, it is transgressive. White supremacy has been founded on the enactment of sadism and sadism is all about deriving pleasure, often sexual, through inflicting pain, humiliation and discomfort[27]. White sadism is therefore all about depriving us of joy. And so, if sadism is central to the reproduction of racist violence then experiencing joy is central to Black liberation[28,29].

TRIPLE CONSCIOUSNESS

'I read a lot and follow some people on Twitter, I educate myself, I try to educate myself on these issues and so I'm aware of like things that suggest unconscious bias, micro-aggressions, macro aggressions [. . .] I've also read a couple of books, for example, *Why I'm no Longer Talking to White People About Race* and, like, she was able to articulate a lot of the things I was feeling.'

The quote is from a research participant, a Black male in his early forties who was interviewed as part of my research on racial trauma. In the quote he shares experience of what he had found helpful in coping with the impact of racism. It reflects the experience of other participants in the study as well as my clinical experience outside the study.

In *The Souls of Black Folk*, W.E.B Du Bois articulates his concept of double consciousness, the internal twoness that is necessary for Black people to adopt as they need to walk through the world inhabiting two sets of consciousness because of racism[30]. Experiencing the world through the eyes of their oppressor and thus their devaluation of Blackness and with the adoption of ways of being in the world and our consciousness, and its own associated worldview and experience. In order to resist racial trauma and to keep our sanity I would suggest that we need to develop an additional level of consciousness to be aware of the two. A level above the primary and secondary levels, which allows us to see conflicts, make sense of them and to remember power is at play.

In my own research, participants were empowered by speaking about their experience. Emerging from the silence was central to the participants' healing journeys. This process relied on having the language, frameworks and conceptual tools to formulate one's experience and, thus, regain a sense of epistemic confidence. This triple-consciousness is required to develop a critical approach to reality and to understand the operationalisation of power and thus see structures of power that underscore the need for **conscientisation**. Conscientisation is the process of becoming a critical thinker and unpacking dominant and oppressive thoughts that result from the cycle of socialisation[31].

LEARNING YOUR POWER

The accessibility of psychological concepts, frameworks and tools has been greatly facilitated by social media, and helps bridge intergenerational conversations. Many of us who now have children have committed to breaking the silence on racial injustice. And the articulation of previously unutterable experiences, transmitting tools to self-affirm and challenge the implicit dominance or hegemony of whiteness. Gaining power is a process of conscientisation, which is to become conscious of the political, socio-economic and cultural oppressive forces underpinning our experience, and gaining the confidence to resist them.

There is a tendency to consider power as an all or nothing game, and to put the psychological burden of atrocities and injustice on Black people. We need to challenge this notion and focus on the losses, the trauma-related effects of white violence on white people. Consequences of racial trauma for white groups, although beyond our remit, need considering too, and not only because they are central to the reproduction of whiteness. But also because focusing on whiteness as a system born out of pathology helps us reject psychological dysfunction. 'White fragility' is a perfect illustration of this psychological vulnerability.

Learned helplessness is a phenomenon that has been observed in both humans and other animals who have endured trauma and mistreatment. When experiencing pain or discomfort, eventually, after enough conditioning, the animal will stop trying to avoid the pain at all. Even if there is an opportunity to truly escape it. The internalisation of power relations means that we also come to expect that there is nothing we can do to change our circumstances and of course this serves whiteness. There are real power asymmetries that exist in the world, but power is shiftable; we have seen over and over that we do have the power to make radical change in our life. Also, remember that there are various kinds of power. It is important to hold on to this reality.

SELF-COMPASSION

Compassion literally means to co-suffer, or to 'suffer with'[32]. It was defined as the feelings that arise in us when we are confronted with the suffering of others, which triggers an urge to alleviate that suffering. Self-compassion can therefore be understood to mean extending compassion to ourselves when we experience suffering or when we feel inadequate, and taking actions to relieve our suffering. American psychologist Kristin Neff, who based her formulation of self-compassion on Buddhist teachings, proposes that self-compassion is composed of three main components, namely: self-kindness, common humanity and mindfulness[32]. She defines self-kindness as being warm towards ourselves when faced with pain and shortcomings rather than ignoring our feelings or resorting to harsh self-criticism. Common humanity involves recognising that suffering and feelings of personal failure are part of what makes us human. They are part of a shared human condition. Finally, Neff conceptualises mindfulness as the act of being balanced towards our emotions and feelings by neither suppressing nor exaggerating them. To Neff, this is about observing with openness and non-judgemental feelings.

This conceptualisation of self-compassion reminds us that 'the very definition of being human means that one is mortal, vulnerable and imperfect'[32]. Current mainstream thinking around self-compassion is colour-blind. I have long been advocating for a more radical use of self-compassion. One that takes our socio-political realities into account and similarly centres resistance. We know that individuals who are poorly treated in the world tend to treat themselves poorly. When we live in hostile environments, we tend to be hostile towards ourselves as we learn to resort to using self-criticism and shame to manage psychological distress and pain. One may say, we internalise the hostility of our environments and come to relate to ourselves in the same way the world has treated us.

Similarly, as we have seen with Black excellence, facing feelings of mediocrity may be particularly painful for Black people because of internalised racism. Connecting to fallibility may be seen to amount to accepting racist notions of inferiority. It may increase our sense of vulnerability in the world. Black people as a group may well be the most forgiving and generous group of human beings on this earth. Yet when it comes to how we treat ourselves (and each other) we can be very unkind. Of course, this is another consequence of internalised racism. By treating ourselves harshly when we are experiencing pain, by not attending to our suffering when we feel inadequate and by silencing these experiences, we disconnect ourselves further from our own humanity, we isolate ourselves. From a more radical socio-political perspective, by treating ourselves harshly, we essentially do the 'master's work': we objectify ourselves and reproduce societal contempt towards Black bodies. Self-compassion helps break the cycle[33,34]. In doing so, it re-engages us to the fullness of our humanity.

Using compassion and self-compassion to relate to each other and ourselves also seems consistent with more Afrocentric worldviews. Striking similarities between the Buddhist conceptualisations of self-compassion and Ubuntu philosophy can be made. Ubuntu is a Zulu term that describes the essence of being human 'Muntu' = 'a human being', 'Ntu' = 'human'. 'Umuntu Ngumuntu Ngabantu' is generally taken to mean we are people because of other people, in other words because we can only exist through other people. And it is the humanity of others that gives ours and vice versa. Being is therefore a process by which we become aware of the us in others and the others in us. Ubuntu places emphasis on the interconnected nature of human experiences or how our internal worlds are inseparable[35]. This African philosophy rests on the belief that every person and every life comes into being through social consciousness, mutuality and connection. Applying Ubuntu in the context of healing and wellness means seeking to actualise these existential and spiritual dimensions as we navigate white supremacy.

SUMMARY

1.

There is a long Black history of resistance that has historically been erased, pathologised or interpreted through a deficiency lens fundamentally reflecting white supremacy's self-protection.

2.

Anti-Blackness assaults our dignity repeatedly and cumulatively. This can lead to racial trauma, experiences of humiliation and can be mitigated by cultivating a Black pride, connecting with beauty and with joy.

3.

Reframing Black excellence and instead aiming to show ourselves kindness and self-compassion can be freeing for Black groups, and as part of that reclaiming our right to be mediocre is reclaiming our unconditional humanity.

4.

Learning to theorise our experience is central to trusting our reality and to making sense of the world. The trusting and naming of our experience is a way to regain a sense of power and agency in the world.

RACE REFLECTIONS

Resisting racism and healing from racial trauma entails our active participation. Resisting is not a passive game. And similarly, in a context of white supremacy, we simply cannot realistically hope to be well, stay well and thrive without dedicating some efforts. This section gives you the opportunity to reflect on resistance and healing to help ensure you have what you need to thrive.

The last part of the book consolidates our learning process and invites you to commit to a self-care routine.

What have you found most troubling in this chapter?

You may want to explore your bodily responses, images and thoughts that came to you and explore what they might take you back to. Please use the Race Reflections reflective model (p.207) to help you.

....

....

....

....

....

There are so many ways to resist and there is no magic formula to survive and thrive within white supremacy. And often those who enact racist violence are also more likely to proclaim what Black resistance should look like.

Thinking about your worldview and white supremacy, what are your expectations of Black people? What do you tend to do when those around you behave in ways that challenge your sense of what resistance should look like?

....

....

....

....

....

Black resistance has an exceptionally long history of condemnation, pathologisation and shaming, which naturally serves the status quo.

Thinking about your own resistance, what actions have led to condemnation, pathologisation and shaming? What has that taught you about white supremacy? How have you changed/adapted as a result?

....

....

....

....

....

Racism robs us of the essence of our humanity.
It often leaves us unable to enjoy the beauty that exists in the world, it distracts us from what feeds the soul and connects us to the world.

Take time to consider what additional opportunities you may create to pay enough attention to beauty in all its manifestations. Art, fashion, nature . . . there is beauty all around us if we pay attention. Taking as much of it as we can is a way to connect to the universe and to find meaning in the world.

....

....

....

....

....

ACTION POINT
CHART YOUR RESISTANCE HISTORY

We discussed how we internalise societal contempt and shaming including messages of dysfunction and pathology in relation to Black resistance, even though we know what the function of these messages is. Remember we are socialised to serve the needs and maintain the comfort of those with more power and we will therefore likely frequently experience discomfort, tension or an internal conflict when we resist.

In order to externalise or challenge the centring of whiteness within ourselves, it is helpful to remember how much as a people we owe to the resistance of our parents, forebears and ancestors.

Your action point: Find out what your resistance history looks like. You may find looking at the history of resistance from those around you, including your parents, inspiring. Similarly, please do some research to be more familiar with how freedom fighters have consistently been ill-treated within white supremacy and how, over time, they have come to be defined as heroes.

FINAL THOUGHTS
THRIVING WHILE BLACK

Navigating the world while Black can be a maze. And there is no doubt that white supremacy inflicts harm and that this harm is often invisibilised. Racial trauma, as we have seen, is complex, it operates at many levels and often affects several generations, who become engaged in repeating histories, unaware that they are fulfilling scripts the world needs them to fulfil.

We have seen that trauma can leave us vulnerable to experiencing helplessness and to believe that we are powerless. In fact, society and white supremacy have much vested interest in us believing that we are.

We are not powerless. And Black lives do matter. Our stories matter.

Powerful Black people have always been feared. Especially when they draw from ancestral wisdom and memory and their hunger for justice and for freedom.

The world depends on us internalising powerlessness and so we may come to fear our own power and thus fear ourselves.

This fear of power is something each of us must confront. And like most of the experiences in the book, it does not sit in isolation from socio-historical contexts. But the fear of our own power and the transformational potential it offers can stand in the way of our liberation, of us centring our needs and acting in a way that sustains us and resists racism.

This is the reason so many of us deny ourselves our creativity and why so many of us leave our gifts unwrapped. We make the decision – conscious or otherwise – not to materialise our potential because of this deep-seated fear.

But we sit at crossroads many times in our lives.

Perhaps even many moments in the day. The direction we take at these junctions is up to us. I hope *Living While Black* has provided enough material, tools and reflections to help some of us to take a different direction or at least to be mindful of our steps. We do have the power to make different choices even as we remain constrained within the violent structures of anti-Blackness.

The freedom to choose direction is power. Where do we go from here? The familiar road? The one that guarantees a degree of safety because of familiarity . . . or do we choose the unknown? Do we take the way of uncertainty, trusting the path laid by our ancestors? Trusting our intuition and our body?

We deserve to be free. And we deserve to thrive. It is time to connect with our power.

GLOSSARY

A

Adverse Childhood Experiences
Adverse childhood experiences (ACEs) is the expression used to refer to traumatic experiences that happen to us before we reach the age of 18. The list of ACEs is varied and includes things like abuse, neglect, bullying, parental trauma or psychological distress, racism . . . ACEs are of interest to clinicians and public health professionals because they can often predict health outcomes and statuses in later life.

African American Vernacular English (AAVE)
African American English (AAE) or Vernacular English (AAVE) or Ebonics is the form of English spoken by Black Americans in the US. It is believed to have connections with languages spoken elsewhere in the Black diaspora, e.g. Jamaica and Nigeria.

Amygdala
The amygdala is the structure in the brain that is almond shaped and located at the base of the brain, one part in each hemisphere. The amygdala is often referred to as the fear centre because one of its primary functions is to activate the fight-or-flight response and modulate the emotional response to threatening stimuli or information.

Anti-Blackness
Anti-Blackness is first and foremost antagonism, hatred or contempt for people racialised as Black because they are Black. Anti-Blackness

is structural, psychological and relational. Anti-Blackness is premised on the alleged 'primitivity' and inferiority of people of African descent and manifests in normalised violence in all domains of functioning for Black people including legally, economically and politically. Anti-Blackness is not only a Black and white binary affair. Non-Black groups equally benefit from anti-Blackness and commonly participate in it.

Anti-racism

Anti-racism is fundamentally any action we deliberately take to dismantle white supremacy. Anti-racism has been defined as the active and deliberate process of identifying and dismantling racism in all its manifestations so that power may be redistributed and shared equitably in society.

Anxiety

Anxiety refers to the condition of being uncomfortable, physiologically or psychologically distressed because of worry. When persistent or interfering with everyday life, feelings of anxiety may require support or signal 'mental health problems'.

Assimilation

Assimilation in the context of immigration or cultural exchanges refers to the process of taking in full the dominant culture, worldview and values at the expense of the culture, worldview or values of one's heritage, ancestry or marginalised group.

Attachment

Attachment refers to the deep and enduring emotional bond between two people characterised by closeness and feelings of security when in the presence of the attachment figure and distress or angst when separated. The first relationship between infant and caregiver is the basis of attachment theory, which sees this relationship as central to an individual's subsequent social, emotional and cognitive development and ability to form stable relationships with others.

Autonomic nervous system

The autonomic nervous system is the part of the nervous system that controls and regulates involuntary physiological processes such as our heart rate, blood pressure and sexual arousal.

B

Black excellence
Black excellence speaks the social process by which the extraordinary achievements of Black people are celebrated and promoted by fellow Black people. It is often believed to uplift Black people and/or disrupt stereotypical expectations. Black excellence has gained much traction on social media, where it continues to be supported via the use of hashtags of the same name.

Black mental health
Black mental health simply refers to the mental health and related issues of those who are racialised as Black.

C

Cisgendered heterosexual (cishet)
Cishet is the abbreviation of cisgender (born in the gender one identifies with) and heterosexual (someone typically attracted to individuals of the opposite sex). The term refers to those who are both cisgender and heterosexual.

Colonialism
Colonialism concerns the use of force, often military, violence or other forms of power by a nation to set up colonies or settlements outside of the borders of one's nations with the aim of increasing the colonising nation's power, influence and/or resources politically, ideologically and/or economically.

Compassion Focused Therapy (CFT)
Compassion Focused Therapy is a form of psychological therapy that harnesses the use of self-compassion to reduce psychological distress linked to self-criticalness and excess shame. It was developed by clinical psychologist Professor Paul Gilbert in the late 1990s and early 2000s and has been subject to many studies, which have evidenced its effectiveness within a range of 'mental health problems'.

Conscientisation

Or 'conscienciser', a term first coined in Frantz Fanon's *Black Skins, White Masks* that describes the development of a critical consciousness that increases an individual's awareness of unjust circumstances, events and relations that have become normalised within daily life by consciously adopting an alternative view of yourself and the world.

Cultural homelessness

Cultural homelessness is a term used to describe the anxiety of not having a cultural home or not belonging to any culture that is commonly experienced among bi-cultural or multi-cultural individuals such as migrants, their children or those of mixed ancestry. The term was coined by psychologist Professor Veronica Navarrete Vivero in the late 1990s and has since generated much interest.

D

Dance Movement Psychotherapy (DMP)

DMP or 'dance movement psychotherapy' is a form of expressive therapy, which uses movement in the form of traditional dances or more subtle forms of movement like yoga and stretching to calm the body and to unlock feelings and emotions trapped within, aiming to help individuals reclaim a connection between actions, words and emotions.

Decolonising

Decolonising knowledge means freeing it from 'accepted' forms of knowing and being that have been shaped, developed and enforced by a colonial power. The decolonising movement seeks to expose and critique systems of colonial power that have shaped the world, bringing other knowledge, perspectives and opinions to the forefront.

Defence mechanism

A psychological strategy that is utilised unconsciously to protect a person from anxiety arising from unacceptable thoughts or feelings or parts of the world/us that are too painful or threatening to our sense of self.

Déracinés (Les)
A French expression that literally translates as 'uprooted'. It is often used as a metaphor to describe immigrants, their children or those who are seen to be removed from their own cultural setting.

Double consciousness
Refers to the internal conflict experienced by marginalised, colonised groups within an oppressive society. First published in Du Bois' *The Souls of Black Folk* to describe the psychological challenge African Americans faced looking at themselves through the eyes of white, racist society.

Double jeopardy law UK
A piece of legislation that provided that an individual could not be prosecuted for the same crime twice. The law was changed in 2005 as part of Sir William Macpherson's recommendations from the inquiry into the Stephen Lawrence murder case.

Drug-induced psychosis
A form of 'psychosis' believed to be induced by drugs.

Dualism
Dualism refers to the philosophical separation of the body and the mind that has long been attributed to French philosopher René Descartes.

E

Embodied/embodiment
We speak of embodiment to describe the connection between emotions and the body, the physical manifestation of feelings through bodily sensations and the way our bodies respond to oppressive socio-political realities.

Epigenetics
Epigenetics is the study of how our behaviours and environment can changes our genes or, more precisely, how genes are expressed.

Epistemic homelessness

Epistemic homelessness is the process in which racially marginalised individuals feel disconnected from their sense of truth, of knowing when their experiences of racism are denied by racially privileged individuals. It is the sense of losing one's truth base or anchor as a direct result of the denial of racism. The framework was developed by psychologist Guilaine Kinouani, the author.

G

Gaslighting

Refers to a kind of emotional abuse in which the perpetrator seeks to gain power over the victim by making them doubt their thoughts, memories or feelings.

Geopolitical

Related to geopolitics or the influence of power in the world order, state to state or international relations. The term was coined by the Swedish political scientist Rudolf Kjellén in the early 20th century.

Goal-striving stress

Is the theory that covers the discrepancy that exists between our aspiration for and achievement of a better way of life, weighted by the subjective probability of success, and the level of disappointment experienced if those life goals are not realised, particularly for people of colour who have to battle for equality, status and position in social structures that exclude them.

Group analysis

Group analysis is both a method of understanding processes and dynamics in groups including social groups and a clinical method to support people who have experienced psychological distress. Group analysis seeks to consider individuals in their family, historical and cultural contexts, and uses networks of communication as the basis for treatment and intervention.

H

Hippocampus
The hippocampus is the part of the brain located in the inner (medial) region of the temporal lobe of the brain. It is implicated in various functions including memory formation, orientation in time and space and the regulation of emotional responses.

Homeness
Here it refers to the feeling of homeliness, being connected to a place that feels like home.

I

Imperialism
Imperialism concerns the use of force, often military, violence or other forms of power by a nation to influence, control or take over other nations usually with the aim of territorial expansion and/or increasing the imperial nation's power, influence and/or resources politically, ideologically and/or economically.

Imposterism or imposter syndrome
Imposterism or imposter syndrome refers to subjective feelings of fraudulence or to the fear of being 'found out' that is experienced by high-achieving marginalised individuals in work settings. The framework was developed in the 1970s by psychologist Drs Pauline Clance and Suzanne Imes, who reasoned that gender norms, sexism and discrimination led to highly capable women feeling like imposters at work. Further research has since established that the phenomenon exists along other axes of oppression.

Inflammation
Inflammation is the body's defence against things that harm it, such as infections, injuries and toxins. When something damages our cells, our body releases chemicals (e.g. cortisol) that trigger a response from the immune system to help us. Stress has been shown to interfere with our body's inflammatory responses.

Intergenerational trauma
Trauma that is transferred between generations. First recognised in children of Holocaust survivors, but widely documented in descendants of slaves, native Americans, war survivors, refugees and survivors of interpersonal abuse.

Intersectionality
Intersectionality is the term coined by Professor Kimberlé Crenshaw as a way of analysing the social world to make visible the particular ways axes of oppression, such as race, gender, social class and so on, do not exist in isolation but shape one another and create particular experiences and forms of structural vulnerabilities.

J

John Henryism
John Henryism refers to a way of coping with racism and racist discrimination by working extra hard to succeed. Sustaining such levels of effort results in a range of negative physiological consequences in African American populations including hypertension. The term was coined by African American epidemiologist Dr Sherman James, in reference to 19th-century African American railroad worker John Henry, who died of physical exertion.

M

Medical model
The term medical model from psychiatrist R. D. Laing refers to the 'set of procedures in which all doctors are trained'. It includes complaint, history, physical examination, ancillary tests if needed, diagnosis, treatment and prognosis with and without treatment. When we think about the medical model in relation to mental health, we mean a perspective or set of ideas that centre the medical origin and management of mental health problems.

Medium secure unit
Psychiatric inpatient treatment facilities and care for adults with complex mental health problems who have been in contact with the criminal justice system and who may present a severe risk to

themselves or others. Research has consistently found that Black groups in the UK are much more likely than any other to be treated within medium secure units.

Mental health

There is no universally agreed definition of mental health and how we define it will say much about our worldview and philosophical beliefs. Many define mental health as the absence of mental health problems, seeing wellness through the prism of the psychiatric classification system or the medical model. Many disagree. Generally, though, it is helpful to think about mental health as our ability to lead fulfilling lives and feel connected to the world and people around us.

Mental Health Act

The Mental Health Act 1983 is a piece of legislation that covers the compulsory treatment and detention of people diagnosed with psychiatric disorders that may put themselves or others at risk. Being detained under the Mental Health Act is sometimes called being 'sectioned' in reference to the different sections of the Act.

Mental health problems

Again, since there is no universally agreed definition of mental health, how we define mental health problems is similarly variable. If we see mental health through the prism of psychiatric classification systems, those meeting criteria for diagnoses such as depression, anxiety or schizophrenia would be deemed to have mental health problems. It is important to remember the criticisms in relation to the Western and individualistic bias in this belief system and understand that there are other ways to think about psychological distress or disturbance (for example, by considering white supremacy as psychological pathology).

Microaggressions

A term coined by African American psychiatrist Dr Chester Pierce to describe the commonplace daily verbal, behavioural or environmental indignities, whether intentional or unintentional, that communicate hostile, derogatory, or harmful racial slights and insults toward people of colour.

Misogynoir

Misogynoir is the combination of two terms: misogyny, the hatred of women, and noir, the French word for Black. Misogynoir therefore describes the anti-Black misogyny that Black women experience. It genders anti-Blackness or racialised misogyny targeted at Black women specifically. The term was coined by Black feminist scholar Moya Bailey in the late 2000s.

N

Neo-colonialism

First coined by Ghana's first president, Kwame Nkrumah, in the early 1960s, 'neo-colonialism' refers to the intrusive (mis)management and continuity of the former coloniser's power through economic, political and educational systems.

Neuroplasticity

Neuroplasticity, or 'neuronal plasticity', refers to the brain's ability to adapt and create new connections between our neurons. We rewire our brains to adapt to new circumstances.

Neuroscientific/Neuroscience

Is the scientific study of the nervous system, which aims to help us understand how the brain works and its fundamental properties.

O

Ontological insecurity

When an event or experience challenges or threatens feelings of safety and security within one's own life or existence.

P

Pan-Africanism

Pan-Africanism is a philosophical belief system and a cultural and political movement that seeks Black liberation through unity, solidarity and connection of people of African descent throughout the world.

Patriarchy
Patriarchy is a social system and way of organising the world that ensures the continuing dominance, privileges and power of those who are men or those deemed 'masculine' and the marginalisation and oppression of women or those deemed 'feminine'. Patriarchy, like all systems of oppression, relies on very strict policing of (binary) gender constructions and on being invisible from those who benefit the most from it.

Place attachment
Emotional bond to place/space, which may be a sense of familiarity, belonging or rootedness in a place defined by cultural history or heritage. Place attachment is attributed to social environment psychologists, Drs Irwin Altman and Setha Low.

Post-colonialism
The term is taken to refer to world order after widespread independence from Western colonialism, the various ways colonialism shaped the world order and the movement that seeks to reclaim and rethink the history and agency of people subordinated under colonialism.

Post-Traumatic Slave Syndrome (PTSS)
A framework created by Dr Joy DeGruy, which highlights the survival strategies adopted by African American communities and other members of the African diaspora to survive chattel slavery and other related racial trauma that are transferred through the generations and remain in operation today.

Post-Traumatic Stress Disorder (PTSD)
Post-traumatic stress disorder (PTSD) is a condition that can develop after an individual has witnessed or been involved in a traumatic event(s). The condition was first recognised in war veterans and has been known by a variety of names, such as 'shell shock'. But it's not only diagnosed in soldiers – a wide range of traumatic experiences can cause PTSD.

Prefrontal cortex

The prefrontal cortex is the part of the brain referred to as the cerebral cortex. The cerebral cortex is the thin layer of the brain that covers its outer part. The prefrontal cortex covers the front of the frontal lobe. Prefrontal cortex functions include our social behaviours as well as our executive functions such as planning, concentrating and making decisions.

Projections

A psychological defence mechanism conceptualised by Sigmund Freud describes the process by which unwanted thoughts, motivations, emotions and impulses are attributed or transferred to another person.

Projective identification

Projective identification is a psychological process or defence by which we take in others' projections (disowned feelings, impulses, fantasies . . .) as though they were ours and behave, feel or think in accordance with them. Projective identification is one of the more complex defence mechanisms with a full theory going back to infant functioning developed by British psychoanalyst Melanie Klein.

Prone position

The prone position is where an individual lies face down with their chest on the ground. The prone position when used in restraint is particularly dangerous and has been linked to high risks of death by asphyxia.

Psychoanalysis

Various theories and clinical and social approaches related to the study and theorisation of the unconscious and the treatment of psychological distress. Psychoanalysis is premised on the existence of an unconscious, a psychic or psychological reservoir of those parts of us or the world we lack awareness of, but which affect our relational and communicational arrangements.

Psychological formulation
Psychologists and especially those who are clinicians speak about formulation when they attempt to make sense of people's presenting difficulties, complaints and problems. Most formulations make connections between the past and the present to better understand what might keep patterns going.

R

Racial identity development
We speak of racial identity development to speak of the process by which we grow in our sense of affiliation, belonging or identification with a racial group.

Respectability politics
Respectability politics is an expression used to refer to the politics of those who are from marginalised groups and who advocate assimilation, decorum and the acceptance and mimicking of dominant values. In the context of race, it means embracing white middle class ways of being and thinking to bring honour, 'to be respectable', to overcome racism.

S

Schizophrenia
Schizophrenia is categorised as a 'severe and enduring' psychiatric condition with a vast array of symptoms, chiefly unusual perceptions or beliefs that are inconsistent with those held in one's socio-cultural group such as seeing or hearing things others don't or believing things others struggle to understand. Schizophrenia belongs to the family of psychoses. Psychoses are mental states characterised by losing touch with reality.

Severe and enduring mental health problems
Describes diagnoses of a mental health condition(s) that are expected or believed to affect a person throughout their lifetime. In the UK they include diagnoses of bi-polar disorder and schizophrenia. They are often opposed to 'common mental health problems',

which are believed to carry less risk and be more easily manageable and treatable and include issues such as 'depression' and 'anxiety'.

Social construct
Social construct(ion)s describes things or concepts that have no 'objective' or 'real' existence except what we as a society and by consensus have decided.

Social inclusion
Is the practice to ensure various groups of people can take part in society fully and to tackle social structures, policies or process that exclude disadvantaged groups.

Stereotype
A stereotype is an over-generalised belief about a particular class or group of people, regardless of its individuals' behaviour.

Structural racism
Structural racism refers to the racism that is embedded within social structures such as schools, the police and/or the military. This form of racism is often hidden and not consciously enacted. It exists because these structures were configured to serve the interests of white groups and as a result disadvantage people of colour through procedures, processes and practices that discriminate at collective level against people of colour.

Structural violence
Structural violence is a term coined by Norwegian sociologist, Johan Galtung, that refers to social structures and economic, political, medical and legal systems that perpetuate inequity through the unequal distribution of power, and which disproportionately affect marginalised groups and communities.

T

The Talk
The Talk refers to the conversation parents have with young Black children to prepare them for racism and in particular the dangers of encounters with the police and other authority figures with a view

to increase their chances of surviving these potentially deadly exchanges.

Telomeres
Telomeres are sections of DNA found at the ends of each of our chromosomes; they help to protect the ends of our chromosomes from damage or fusing with nearby chromosomes. With age or stress telomeres have been shown to shorten.

U

Unconscious bias
Unconscious bias, also known as implicit bias, refers to the underlying attitudes, prejudices and stereotypes we hold towards people that evade our conscious awareness, but which still influence the behaviour and treatment of these groups.

W

Whiteness
Whiteness is a social system that ensures the production and reproduction of the dominance and privileges of people racialised as white.

Whitening the race (racial whitening)
Racial whitening is an ideology centred around the idea that Black inferiority or 'the Black problem' could be resolved over successive generations by 'breeding' exclusively with white people. It was believed that over time such selective and racially motivated breeding would lead to the genetic, cultural and social improvement and ultimately the disappearance of the Black race. Although the ideology is more strongly associated with Latin America, it has been found in parts of the Caribbean.

YOUR RADICAL SELF-CARE PLAN

Self-care has been co-opted and misused. It has become synonymous with consumerist images of white women pampering themselves, sanitising its radical origins. The politics of self-care finds its origin within the racial struggle, and it became a central part of movements for justice, liberation and equality. Although the radical origins of self-care lie firmly in the civil rights movement, it was women and in particular Black feminist scholars who made it an integral part of their praxis, as evidenced by the following Audre Lorde quote, possibly the most well-known quote on self-care: 'Caring for myself is not self-indulgence, it is self-preservation, and that is an act of political warfare.'

To Lorde, self-care is an act of defiance. Indeed, when systems are designed to harm you, if not kill you, and you insist on staying alive and well, you are challenging the very fabric of society and the social order. The quote from Lorde is extracted from *A Burst of Light*, a book she wrote shortly after being diagnosed for the second time with cancer. This personal context adds poignancy and depth to her political call. Her life was under assault from patriarchy, homophobia and racism. Her life was in peril not only from these systems but from cancer. The threat of death was real, and so was the yearning for loud and powerful survival. So loud it still resonates.

Lorde's self-care call is also a call for self-love at a time when Black bodies were despised and subjected to overt hateful violence. In this context, self-love is also about Black love. Self-care is love for Black people. Practising self-care within a white patriarchal society screamed Black Lives Matter well before we started saying Black

Lives Matter. Audre Lorde thus reconnects us with the intended direction of self-care. Self-preservation. And specifically, self-preservation as political warfare. Today things are arguably different but the struggle for racial justice is ongoing in the United States, in the UK, in France and in most Western nations. It may look different, but it is the same struggle in the Global South.

As I write, Black people are, it feels, under constant assault. Social media means images of dead Black bodies are constantly doing the rounds in front of our eyes. Drowning *en masse* in the Mediterranean because of anti-Black border control. As well as dying disproportionately of COVID-19. Since we witnessed the video of the suffocation of George Floyd protests are ongoing and racial inequalities are recurrently making headlines as topics of conversation. Rarely ever though as topics of action. And, in the midst of this normalised violence, we are invited to 'debate' our humanity and welfare again and again.

Most of us aspire to be the best version of ourselves and to at the very least survive. But we need to be bold and aspire to do more. To thrive and to be well. Practising self-care is essential to buffer the impact of racism and racial trauma on us, which is a pre-requisite to living a good life while Black. The present plan has been designed to encourage and support these efforts. It aims to encourage you to reflect and to set goals or aspirations in relation to your welfare and psychological development as a Black person.

The plan is focused on your body, mind, soul and their interconnection. It also seeks to help you connect to who you are as a whole and connect to the world around you to ultimately support your growth. You are invited to engage with the suggested activities regularly – ideally, if you can, use the journal from your first action point. Frequencies are suggested. Please feel free to vary them, for example increase usage during times of stress.

1: NURTURE YOUR BODY (DAILY)

Our body is the primary tool of resistance. As we have seen throughout this book, racism has deleterious effects on both our body and our mind. We as a community can be rather neglectful of our physical health. We therefore neglect our main tool of resistance, our main boundary, our main refuge.

Although this relative cultural neglect of our physical health must be located within a context of structural racism, intergenerational trauma and internalised racism, many of us need to relearn our relationship with our bodies and start to show both gratitude and appreciation for them keeping us alive and functioning in the midst of racial violence. A negative attitude towards our bodies encourages us to neglect, abuse and harm ourselves and reproduces societal contempt toward Blackness.

This may require a shift in our attitude and treatment of ourselves, including the value we place on our body. The start of this growth plan invites you to reflect on possible devalued stories you may have internalised about your body. They may be related to Eurocentric standards of beauty, racial stereotypes or be a response to repeated experiences of denigration. In this section you are invited to relate to your body with kindness, gratitude and love. You may want to use this space to address your body and write loving words to it directly e.g. 'you have continued to help me despite . . .' or pay special attention to specific body parts you want to start to engage with in a more loving way. Some people find expressly asking their body forgiveness helpful.

NURTURE YOUR BODY

2: DO A 'JOY INVENTORY' (WEEKLY)

Black joy is the ultimate tool of defiance. It can also be the most difficult practice to engage in and to sustain within white supremacy and thus in the midst of Black pain. There are various reasons society finds Black joy intolerable, but part of the reason is that it humanises us. It renders us complex and multi-dimensional beings capable of the full range of emotions.

Experiencing joy and pleasurable activities acts as a strong buffer against hopelessness and low mood. In psychological jargon this is referred to as 'behaviour activation'. Please take some time to write down all the things that bring joy and commit to doing them regularly. Commitment without a plan however is like travelling without a passport. It reduces the chances of us getting far.

Therefore, in a second part of this activity, plan pleasurable activities you have identified in your list. What is planned is much more likely to get done.

Make sure you do a little bit of that joyful stuff every day. Set alarms on your phone, write them in the journal and make time to do them. This is also part of reprogramming our relationship with our body and recalibrating our brains.

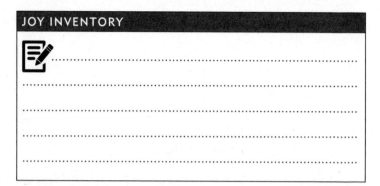

JOY INVENTORY

3: CHECK YOUR ACHIEVEMENTS (MONTHLY)

When we experience racism, it is easy to forget what we have achieved and become consumed with self-doubt, feelings of inadequacy and/or powerlessness. The reality is that as we go through difficult experiences, we also learn key skills and strategies to navigate the society that has been handed to us. Make time to remember victories big and small. This will help increase your sense of agency and mastery, but also remind you to learn from your experience.

Please complete a record of your greatest achievements. They can be little things or large things. Things you do for yourself and things you do for others, professional or community related activities. You may want to ask two or three people you trust. It would be helpful if at least one of these people is not related to you. Ask them to list your greatest achievements as they see them. Compare the information you obtained to the achievements you came up with. Add any information missing. Reflect on any discrepancy; many of us tend to minimise our achievements. Regularly revisit this list and add achievements as they arise.

ACHIEVEMENTS

4: DO A QUALITY INVENTORY (MONTHLY)

Once you have completed your achievement checklist, it will be much easier for you to see your gifts, talents and the aptitudes you possess. Many of us find it difficult to tolerate our giftedness. But it is important that we learn to take this in. In a racist society, it is natural and understandable to internalise racist fantasies or stereotypes that are projected onto us and to define ourselves in a way that is consistent with others' prejudices and expectations. Over time some of us may lose sight of what we're good at.

As with the previous activity, make a list, but this time of what you're good at. There should be at least seven gifts, talents or aptitudes.

Make it a habit to revisit this list too, particularly when you are going into spaces where you are underrepresented, or before an important evaluation. Doing a quality inventory can be a helpful way to reconnect ourselves to all that we have to offer to the world and to build our self-esteem. A higher self-esteem has been found to mitigate the negative impact of racist violence. Maintaining a healthy self-esteem is therefore important work to engage in.

INVENTORY

5: CONNECT WITH BLACK PRIDE (MONTHLY)

What is it about being Black that you love, if not adore? Despite racism, few of us would swap racial background given the choice. This tells us that we know that Blackness entails beauty and gifts and that there are plenty of things we would not change about Living While Black, for the world. What makes you feel grateful for being Black? What about Blackness brings you a sense of pride? When do you most feel proud about being Black? Let us try to document those things for YOU.

It is important that you define for yourself what brings you pride; this may be quite different to those around you and that is okay. This is not about agreement or consensus. This is about your personal connection or affiliation with Blackness. About your personal relationship with Blackness and how you experience and perceive it.

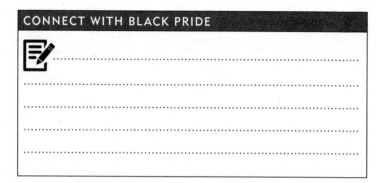

6: MAP YOUR LINEAGE

Try to locate yourself in terms of family lineage as far back as you can go. Find out as much as possible about your relatives on both sides of your family; if possible, do a family tree. As you do, you may also want to think about the skills and traits people have in common and those you share with others. What relationships are strong? Which are weak? Where does trauma lie? Some of us who by reason of adoption, estrangement or other separation cannot complete this task about our biological families may want to use our chosen or adopted families to do this. In this case it may be helpful to consider and rank closeness on three levels using circles.

Draw a circle and put yourself in it. People you add in that first circle would be those you are closest to. Outside this circle draw a second circle, and put in this people in your chosen family who matter to your welfare but who you feel less close to. Finally, in the final circle, put the names of those who are members of your chosen or adopted family but who you feel the least connected to. Think about traits, attributes, personality, life experiences that people have in common in these three circles and those you share or may not share. Map anything that may be relevant such as interests, professions and personality and relate this material to you. See the patterns that emerge in this physical representation of your home. Once your circle is completed please revisit it two to three times a year; update it as appropriate. We suggest you place it in a private area you can easily access.

MAP YOUR LINEAGE

7: LEARN ABOUT BLACK HISTORY
(ALL YEAR)

The framework of Black history remains a controversial one. There is no history that is uniquely Black and what we construct as Black history is often recounted through a white European gaze. Nonetheless, here we use the expression to refer to historically significant events and processes when it comes to our identity and worldview; as Black people so many events and stories have been deformed and twisted to maintain the illusion of white supremacy. There is so much about Black history we do not know about because of systematic erasure and revisionism. Finding out more through our own research and reading is a lifelong journey. But it is a journey of self-discovery too. However, it is important that we see Blackness as being located within specific socio-historical and economic contexts and remember those most likely to be disappeared under the same hierarchies of power and proximity to the white European master.

Ask yourself: What would I like to know more about? What knowledge have I been deprived of? If I were writing a history book what chapter might I first want to write about? What do I need to know about history to better understand my lived experience today?

This section invites you to make a discovery plan and a research plan about Black history. The above questions will guide your research and help you set priorities.

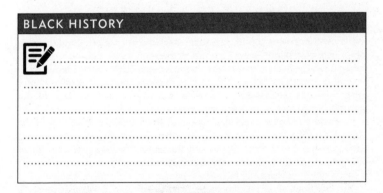

BLACK HISTORY

8: FOSTER BELONGING (MONTHLY)

Cultural homelessness is said to occur when we feel neither quite at home within the culture of our parents or heritage nor in that of the country we were born or reside in. Often, this is due to repeated experiences of marginalisation, discrimination or Othering. It is the sense of not feeling quite at home anywhere. Cultural homelessness can leave us feeling vulnerable, unprotected and forever in search of belonging. This cultural alienation and yearning are central to the experiences of many Black people. And it could most definitely be a manifestation of racial trauma.

There are various ways to increase our sense of belonging. Affirmations can work for some e.g. 'I belong', 'I have as much right to be here as others' or again 'my forebears built this country'. For others, it may be helpful to remember that experiences of cultural homelessness are a function of our social location more than they are a reflection of our actual right of abode. People with more social power usually struggle much less with entitlement in relation to space and land, irrespective of how illegitimate their claims might be. Use this space to note the things (or people) that remind you that you belong. Revisit and add to this monthly.

FOSTER BELONGING

....

....

....

....

....

9: CONNECT TO YOUR HERITAGE

We know that having a positive relationship with our ancestry and heritage often acts as a buffer when it comes to experiences of racism. It can truly help provide protection to ourselves and increase our sense of homeness. It is thus so important that we feel a sense of connection to Blackness and/or Africanness as well as where possible the culture and heritage of our parents, grandparents and/or forebears.

What do you know about this aspect of your identity and heritage? The way of thinking, the way of feeling, the food, the music, the communities etc . . . What can it teach you about the world? About resistance, about love, about harmony, about spirituality? Seeking to better understand various aspects of this heritage will help develop your sense of connection to it.

You are entitled to reclaim these cultural ties and develop a sense of ownership. However, as you engage or re-engage with your cultural heritage, please use a critical lens, and remember we are socialised to assess non-Western cultures via a Eurocentric gaze . . . whenever possible check your findings with relevant communities.

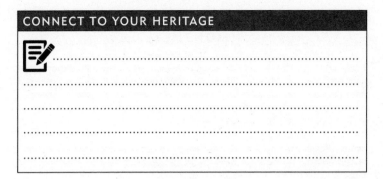

CONNECT TO YOUR HERITAGE

10: CONNECT WITH NATURE (WEEKLY)

Most non-Western worldviews have historically held connection with nature as central to wellness and social harmony. This is the case for traditional African beliefs too. Although these beliefs have long been belittled within Eurocentric thought, plenty of research is now documenting how connecting with nature fosters human flourishing and enhances our social, psychological and relational life. Exploring or experiencing nature, living near nature, or even viewing nature have all been shown to have positive effects on our minds, bodies and social interactions. What is even more encouraging is that nature can help us process trauma and increase our wellbeing. Therefore as Black people reclaiming nature is important to our resistance and self-care. Our ancestors are part of nature. They are in the air we breathe, the ground we walk on, they are all around us and in us.

There are several ways we can get closer to nature even for those of us stuck in urban jungles and with concrete and cement as landscape. Here are a few suggestions: can you visit a green space regularly? If not, can you grow something? Even if this is only on your windowsill and in a tiny pot? Nurturing a plant and growing a seed is one of the cheapest ways to connect with nature and greenery. Failing all these you may be left to have to use the power of your imagination by making efforts to visualise natural landscapes such as forests, parks or beaches and making it a habit to create a green corner in your mind. Nature-based relaxation aids can be easily found online or you may simply wish to obtain paintings, pictures or photographs of nature.

CONNECT WITH NATURE

11: MAKE INTERGENERATIONAL LINKS (MONTHLY)

If this is possible for you, consider strengthening connections with the land(s) of your heritage and ancestry. Remember there are many among us within our communities who act as bridges between our ancestry and the present and may hold some of this history. Do you have conversations with the elders in your family and/or community? Seek to connect with them regularly; they are a rich source of experience and invaluable living archives that we tend not to utilise. Seek connection in their experiences. Hear and record their stories. Nature may also be used here to forge these ancestral connections. Here is a possible activity to mindfully connect with our ancestors through nature: Stand barefoot on grass or soil; as you do, focus on the connection between you and the earth. Take in all the sensation that you can grasp through your senses. The colour, the smell, how the meeting of your being and the earth feel.

Now visualise communities that came before you and walked that very same earth, smelled the very same grass and stared at the same soil. We share these elements; nature is also a mechanism of connection with the past. By deeply connecting with earth, soil and nature's elements we are also connecting with our ancestors. If you have the possibility of going to the land(s) of your heritage or ancestry and no longer live there, another suggestion is to bring back a little soil if you can. The act of feeling, smelling that soil when you are away, can connect you to your history and ancestry.

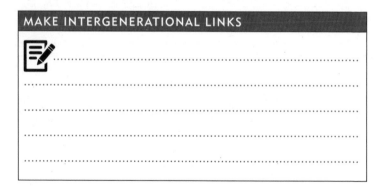

MAKE INTERGENERATIONAL LINKS

12: FEED YOUR SOUL (WEEKLY)

We are a highly musical people. We have used music through the centuries to share stories, pass on heritage, to build community and fight racial oppression. It is this extraordinarily rich and complex history that is revealed through the way we move our bodies to music and the way our soul becomes enlivened through rhythms. Music is a deeply spiritual practice that allows us to reach a different experiential field. We can facilitate this process by using drumming.

Drumming has long been used to promote healing and the expression and processing of grief and trauma throughout the Global South and in Africa. It has been used for millennia to improve physical, mental and spiritual health. Again, we have increased evidence that drumming particularly when done in community alleviates trauma-related distress. Engaging in drumming therefore fulfils a varied purpose. It may connect us to our spiritual self, connect us to the motherland and help heal trauma. If drumming is not accessible, consider joining a community dance group, ideally a form of dance that directly connects you to your heritage (the choice is vast . . .).

FEED YOUR SOUL

13: NURTURE YOUR COMMUNITY (WEEKLY)

Whiteness, as we have seen, has eroded our community and ancestral ties. Our personal healing cannot be separated from the healing of our community. We are so interdependent that we cannot exist or do well if we have no community or if our community is hurting. This is the spirit of the African philosophy of Ubuntu. We are because you are. Our fate and our wellness cannot be separated. Looking after our community is looking after ourselves too.

Furthermore, one of the most important things you need to think about is how you are going to sustain yourself. None of us can do this self-care alone, at least not effectively. Social support is incredibly important to survive racism. Vital, even. Not only will it act as an additional buffer, but we do know that Living While Black leaves us vulnerable to chronic exclusion, ostracisation and for many of us further marginalisation. Of course, risks are not equally distributed. Your positionality and the social power this affords you can reduce or increase the above risks. Nonetheless these risks exist for everyone: nurturing your community is nurturing yourself.

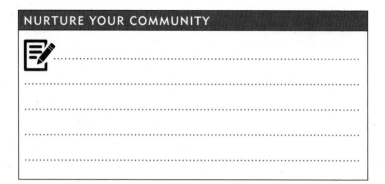

NURTURE YOUR COMMUNITY

14: GET ORGANISED (MONTHLY)

Pursuing anti-racism and any kind of liberation requires becoming fully aware of oppressive systems, their impact on individuals and on groups. But anti-racism is more than an intellectual pursuit. Some say it is a verb. It is a 'doing'. Engaging in activities aimed at dismantling white supremacy and in fact, all systems of oppression, takes critical reflection and action. This is what is commonly referred to as 'praxis'. Social organising fulfils various goals. It brings people together and creates a sense of community and togetherness around shared concerns. It shares and collectivises the responsibility for social change. It helps us connect, see one another, and thus humanise us all. It allows us to regain a sense of power and keep the bigger picture – the structural picture – in mind.

There are various ways to work towards social change and there are various ways to do social organising. For this activity, get familiar with groups and communities working towards racial justice or equality that are in operation at grassroots level within your locality. Connect with them. Try to have conversations with at least one of them. Think about ways you may be able to support them or contribute to their efforts, but also get support from them.

GET ORGANISED

PSYCHOLOGICAL TOOLS

RACE REFLECTIONS REFLECTIVE MODEL

Reflectivity may be taken as the process of learning from our experience to grow, develop and gain new insights into ourselves, others and the world. Several reflective practice models exist. Few if any pay attention to embodied data, yet, as we engage in reflection it is important to remember the body, given the potentially triggering impact of race-based material. Race Reflections' reflective model supports a holistic engagement with knowledge and data.

We ask that each time you are exposed to new information, particularly information that challenges your worldview, you pause to engage in the reflective cycle below. This will help you process information more deeply and engage with your body, cognitively as well as emotionally.

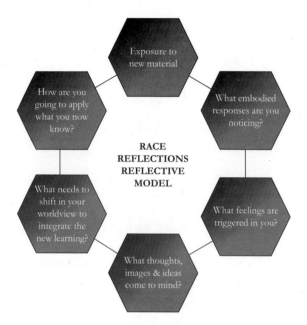

RACE REFLECTIONS INTERSECTING IDENTITY STAR

Race Reflections Intersecting Identity Star is a tool designed to encourage reflections on positionality. Positionality refers to where we stand within social structures and the impact of the various axes of oppression that shape our social identities and worldview as well as access to power. These axes include (but are not limited to) race, class, gender, gender expression, sexual orientation, religion and ability status, as well as all their intersections.

The point of this tool is to help you visualise some of the most common social identities and their intersections, reflect on both privileged and marginalised identities and approach racial trauma and racism in a way that is nuanced and considers the multiple identities we all occupy.

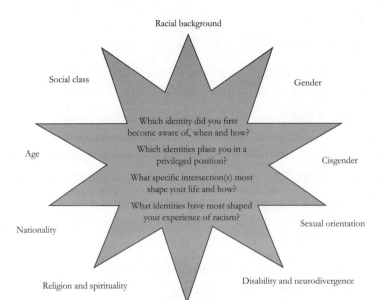

Racial background

Social class

Gender

Age

Cisgender

Which identity did you first
become aware of, when and how?

Which identities place you in a
privileged position?

What specific intersection(s) most
shape your life and how?

What identities have most shaped
your experience of racism?

Nationality

Sexual orientation

Religion and spirituality

Disability and neurodivergence

Immigration status

VISUALISING SAFETY

Feeling unsafe in the world is associated with trauma and while we can never feel completely safe within white supremacy nor would it be adaptive, feeling constantly alert to possible dangers is not only exhausting, it can deeply affect our physical and psychological health. We need, however difficult it might be, to learn to switch off and find safety whenever we can.

Learning to practise relaxation is a fundamental skill to mitigate the stress of racism.

There are various scripts that exist online for the purpose of relaxation. You are free to use them and play around with them and shift them in a way that allows you to make them your own.

Initial instructions

1. Find a place that is safe and quiet and where you expect not to be interrupted.

2. In that space, make yourself as comfortable as you can. You may adopt any position. Choose one that does not make you feel self-conscious or strain your body.

3. Close your eyes, if you feel safe enough to do so. If you do not feel safe enough, lower your head and gaze.

4. Take a few deep breaths. It helps to pay close attention to the air entering and leaving your body and to your tummy (rather than your chest) rising and falling.

Script

You are about to travel to a place of safety and these directions will help you get there.

The first thing we need to do is find an image or place of safety. It may be real or imagined. It may be a place you have always wanted to go or a place you have visited. Many find visualising a beach, a forest or a familiar room helpful, but it could be anywhere.

When you have this place in your mind, visualise yourself entering it calmly and noting instantly the relaxing effect that being in this place of peace has upon your whole being.

As you start to connect with safety, take a few more deep breaths and with each breath, allow your body to take in the safety and peace all around you.

In order to help your body, take in as much safety as you can. You now want to focus on all your senses. It does not matter where you start. You may want to first concentrate on the sound you hear in this place of safety. What does safety sound like? Pay minute attention.

Once you have spent enough time imagining the sound and hearing it in your mind, you may focus on the colours. What does safety look like? Pay minute attention.

Once you have spent enough time taking in colours in your place of safety, you may focus on the sensations on your skin, the texture, the warmth, anything you can perceive through your sense of touch.

Once you have spent some time taking in the sensations on your skin, you may want to focus on smell and even taste.

Use at least three different sensory modalities to help your body connect to safety and experience it for five to ten minutes.

Once you feel relaxed, take a few more deep breaths, and prepare to exit your place of peace and safety, remembering you carry this place within you and that you can return to it whenever you want or need.

Open your eyes.

Tips

Remember that it is often more helpful to practise visualisation and relaxation regularly so that it becomes habitual and more easily called on when needed.

There is really no right or wrong way to practise this script. You may initially struggle to remain focused and may find that your mind starts to wander places you do not want to go to; if that is the case simply refocus your attention onto your breath then gently re-invite your mind onto one of your senses.

You may initially struggle to do five to ten minutes or to use all sensory modalities. And that is perfectly fine; with practice you will most likely get there.

Visualisation is not for everyone, although I rarely meet people who find it unhelpful.

THE GLASS OF DIRTY WATER

We have seen that racial trauma can cause us to experience high levels of shame. We have also seen that shame serves various functions in society and that it is a by-product of white supremacy.

I use the 'glass of dirty water' exercise in therapy. Many patients find it helpful when reconsidering their relationship with shame and in locating it within socio-political contexts.

You are invited to get a full glass of water and simply place it somewhere in your field of vision, ideally at eye level. Imagine the water is dirty.

In therapy, I use questions such as: when was the glass of dirty water first handed to you? How full was the glass? How much of it did you drink? What did the water do to you? How much of it are you still drinking today? Who has been handing you the glasses? Who tends to be handed glasses of shame socially? In situations of abuse of power, who hands who the glass? What makes people more likely to drink the water and why might that be so?

The choice of the word 'handed' here is purposeful. It aims to establish a boundary or distance between shame and us as people who experience it. It aims, too, to highlight the possibility of agency, since something that is handed to us symbolically can be handed back or refused. Finally, it reflects that while shame can so easily be taken in, it can similarly easily be shared.

Specific examples may be discussed to highlight the role of racialised and gendered hierarchies in the distribution of shame. So I might ask, in situations of gendered violence (against women) who tends to be handed the glass? Or again when it comes to economic exploitation, who drinks the water? In colonial situations etc . . . And, knowing what we know, how might we respond to being handed the glass? Who does the water belong to?

Many people find that water has a grounding effect and perhaps, too, it helps to bring the socio-political into the room in a way that is visual and reversible. If you feel up to it, intentionally pour the water down the drain simply to symbolise you resisting shame that does not belong to you. Feel free to repeat this activity each time you struggle with race-based shame.

THE P.O.W.E.R. FRAMEWORK

As we have seen, trauma deeply affects our physiology and renders us more likely to be reactive or triggered in situations where we feel discriminated against. The P.O.W.E.R. framework exists to manage physiological response and increase our sense of agency and confidence. P.O.W.E.R. stands for Prepare, Observe, Wait, Exhale and Resist.

Prepare: When it comes to navigating challenging and possibly hostile spaces, preparation is key. Preparation gives us the chance to anticipate and rehearse possible difficulties, challenges and struggles. These rehearsals increase our sense of readiness and thus confidence, which in turn is likely to increase our agility. Preparation might include anticipating tricky interactions, unwelcome comments and/ or microaggressions and visualising or rehearsing responses.

Observe: An important skill for us to try to master is the art of observing. Here you are invited to observe what is going on in your body, how you are physiologically responding to the space. Next, pay attention to what is going on at interaction level e.g. body language, language used, space and airtime taken. Then elevate your observations by identifying power in relation to positionality but also to the local context e.g. organisational seniority. Once you have a clear sense of where power lies, pay close attention to how it is manifesting in the interaction between people and in relation to you. You may start to observe scripts, patterns, games. Observing is fundamental to formulating what is going on and therefore theorising our lived experience.

Wait: Our tendency to react when we see or experience injustice can be explained physiologically. And while there are plenty of situations when reacting will be appropriate and helpful, in many situations it may deprive us of time to strategise. Think about what the safest or most effective way may be to respond or resolve a problem and simply increase your behavioural choices. For many of us, waiting will allow us to consider all options available.

Exhale: The invitation to exhale (and of course inhale) is a reminder to actively and deliberately work on relaxation in order to help reduce possible anxiety symptoms. Re-centring our body via our breath is a helpful way to bring our physiology back to baseline, not only to minimise 'flight-or-fight' responses, which increase the likelihood of reactiveness, but to help ensure the optimal environment for our cognitive abilities. It helps ensure we can think, reason, plan, concentrate and strategise as effectively as possible.

Resist: At this stage you will be in a much stronger position to resist safely and effectively. A reminder that resistance takes various forms. Sometimes you may decide that silence is the best course of action, having taken all circumstances into consideration. Sometimes you will decide that silence is not an option and you will challenge or confront what was said or done straight away. Alternatively, you may decide that you need more time to seek support and organise. What matters here is that you have consciously thought about what the most suitable course of action may be rather than simply reacted because you were triggered in the moment.

FORMULATING RACIAL DYNAMICS IN GROUPS

This framework uses group analytic ideas to help you make sense of race-based difficulties you may come across in institutional settings and in the workplace.

1. **What is the problem?**
   Often in cases of racial bullying or institutional violence, acts of racial bullying or marginalisation act as cover for some anxiety-provoking but unnamed problem or disturbance. Revisit the story of Julie as an illustration (p.77). Your first question is, what is the real problem?

2. **Who is involved who is present, and who is involved who is not present?**
   Linked to the above, when we experience racial trauma or racist violence we may come to believe we are the problem, or that it is us or only us who

need to change to make ourselves acceptable. It is important to reframe issues of ownership, so as not to internalise the scapegoat role. Remind yourself this is a GROUP problem, and the entire group is involved.

3. **What are the payoffs?**
There will always be gains, conscious or otherwise, for group violence, conflict or dysfunction. Sometimes it is the pure gratification of sadistic impulses. Usually power games are involved. Think about what these payoffs may be in your situation.

4. **And what histories are being reproduced?**
When a person of colour experiences racism within social structures, it is helpful to link their experience to past abusive treatment (theirs, but also those of the group they may belong to) so that possible historical scripts, including parental traumatic histories, may become visible, addressed and sometimes processed. Seeing those patterns can help us to move differently, to disrupt the script and to maximise the chances of a different outcome.

RESISTING WHITE PROJECTIONS

This tool uses psychoanalytic ideas to help us resist white projections. Projection is a psychological defence that entails displacement. With projection we displace feelings we are not prepared to own onto an external object or person. Introjection is what can happen when we are at the receiving end of 'projection'. When we introject the projections of others, as we have seen, we identify with them and specifically their fantasies, wishes and other psychological material. It is a normal process to introject or internalise the psychological world of others – particularly when they hold authority or power in our life. And here lies the problem of internalised racism, or the harm in introjecting the racist messages that we swim in.

To build our resistance to racism and racial trauma we need to build stronger psychological boundaries, so that they are less (only less, and not never) vulnerable to the internalisation of racist violence.

A central tenet of psychoanalysis is that 'insight' is healing and liberating. Insight involves making conscious what may be unconscious and thus naming what may be going on e.g. what may be projected onto us. This act of externalisation can reduce identification with the projected material.

It is likely that such insight will not be sufficient in averting harm within a white supremacist context. However, combined with other interventions, the above psychoanalytic and group analytic formulations can be extremely helpful in buffering the impact of racism on us.

A suggested visualisation exercise

Visualising your skin pores as dilatable and retractable may be a helpful metaphor to represent openness, exposure and vulnerability to foreign invasion. With this activity, you are invited to connect with your skin, the different sensations you feel, then to imagine your pores opening when they are safe and closing when they are unsafe or in vulnerable situations. If you prefer, visualising a flower or any fragile object that can open and close for self-protection can be helpful. Some people find visualising themselves to be in a protective bubble helpful too. Play around with various metaphors and see what works better for you.

NAVIGATING WHITENESS AT WORK

The whiteness at work formulation is a basic tool anyone experiencing racism at work may use. It is questions-based and designed to be simple and accessible. The aims of the tool are to:

1. Make sense of oppressive situations by seeing connections, links and patterns. Formulating and conceptualising racism/oppression is one of the most powerful methods to retain a sense of agency and power when we experience racism.

2. Promote some psychological boundaries and increase our capacity to see the situation in its entirety/from above thus helping us strategise. Racism is a significant stressor. When under stress, our capacity to plan, think clearly and problem solve is often significantly impaired. A helicopter view of the situation can help us problem solve more effectively and stops us from becoming too activated or triggered, and therefore reduces the likelihood of psychological injury/ trauma.

3. Externalise the problem. Once more, strong structural and psychological factors that promote victim-blaming in situations of abuse of power exist. Further, experiences of racism can quickly hook onto past trauma/abuse and/or psychological

'vulnerabilities', increasing their wounding potential. Again, our best defence here is to externalise.

A basic formulation may thus be useful when both navigating and making sense of whiteness at work. The framework is not designed to promote any course of action but aims to encourage reflection and self-care.

Choose your strategies

This tool may be useful both to those affected by racism and those working to support victims/targets.

The framework: basic questions

1. What is the main narrative/discourse? Ask yourself . . .
   What is going on here that sounds typical/predictable?
   What is causing me distress/discomfort? (trust your experience)
   What seems beyond the individuals concerned?

2. How is whiteness being reproduced here? Ask yourself . . .
   What tropes can I recognise?
   What stereotypes are being used?
   What structural inequalities are engaged/perpetuated?

3. Who are the agents of whiteness? Ask yourself . . .
   Who is actively reproducing whiteness?
   Who is passively/inadvertently reproducing whiteness?
   Are there any agents that may be/appear unwilling? (consider using them in question 5)

4. Tactics/devices in use. Ask yourself . . .
   What devices are being used to exclude/Other?
   What is/are the function(s) of those tactics/devices?
   What is the impact of any tactic used (on me and
   on others)?

5. Navigational and resistance strategies. Ask
   yourself . . .
   In relation to the function(s) of the devices in use,
   what strategies are available to me to buffer/
   counteract?
   What support is available to me – internally and
   externally?
   What/who do I already know, that I could summon
   to help me navigate here?

   You may want to organise this information in a table.
   Reflect on your answers.

   Discuss them with others you trust and more
   importantly, derive a plan of action based on what you
   want to achieve in your current situation and the
   support you have. Remember, white supremacy is
   beyond you and it is beyond me too.

WORKING WITH RACIAL TRAUMA

Blackness Centred Compassion therapy

In 2017 I developed the Blackness Centred
Compassion model to incorporate the power of self-
compassion to our structural realities. The model has
at its core the socio-political and historical origin of

racial trauma, how we cope, the impact on us trying to survive in a white supremacist culture and all social functions. It also acknowledges the impact of unsafeness or recurrent stressors in the creation of shame and self-criticism as ways of self-relating because within self-compassion frameworks, the centrality of axes of oppression e.g. racism in creating feelings of unsafeness has received little attention.

The model is a way to make sense of or formulate race-based difficulties.

It links race-based shame and racial trauma to the intergenerational context, to personal histories of resistance and aims to help us understand and explain survival or coping strategies that have been adopted in the context of white supremacy. The point of the model is to foster connection between the 'here and now' and the 'there and then' in a way that centres the experience of racism.

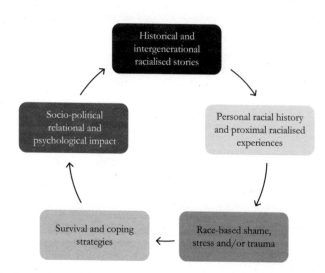

Blackness Centred Compassion Therapy Formulation (Kinouani, 2018)

Historical and Intergenerational (racialised stories)

This covers both historical and family stories related to racism and oppression. They may include how you have been impacted upon by slavery and colonialism or migration, your parents', grandparents' and great-grandparents' experiences. Any related story you are aware of that may have shaped your worldview.

Key question to reflect on:

What have your learnt about the world, others and about yourself from intergenerational stories?

Personal racial histories and 'proximal' experiences (of racism). It would be impossible to remember every single instance of racism we have experienced. We will likely all have stories that have felt more significant and formative.

Key question to reflect on:

What have you learnt about the world, others and about yourself from these experiences?

Race-based shame or racial trauma

This section of the model invites you to reflect on possible trauma and/or shame. We have seen that shame is central to trauma experiences but that it is a difficult emotion to own, even though this shame is largely projected onto us. You may find it helpful to revisit the table of signs and manifestation in Chapter 2.

Key question to reflect on:

What has been the impact of these experiences on how you view and relate to you and Black people?

Survival and coping strategies

Taking all that you have been exposed to and the messages this might have left you with about the world, we know that, as all living organisms do, we have adapted to our environment to survive, although adaptation may look different in different people based on what they have learnt about survival. For example, if I have learnt that I must work twice as hard to avoid racism, workaholism may be my coping strategy. If I have learnt that African features are less valued and should make me feel ashamed, I may seek to attempt to 'Europeanise' my appearance.

Key question to reflect on:

What have been my survival and coping strategies?

Socio-political, relational and psychological impact

Of course, any survival or coping strategies we adopt will have consequences. Some will be desired, and some will be unwanted. For example, if I distance myself from my Blackness to survive, this may compound my sense of inferiority or shame, reproduce whiteness socio-politically and impact my relationships. I may attempt to avoid close relationships with Black people or I may be critical of those who choose to connect with their Blackness in a way that is more Afrocentric.

Key question to reflect on:

What has been the impact of my coping and survival strategies on me psychologically, on my relationships with others and on white supremacy?

The point of the model is not to tell you how to survive white supremacy. Instead it is to help you contextualise how you operate in society as a result of racism and to reflect on the impact with a view to either showing yourself self-compassion and/or how you may have needed to operate. Then if you so wish, attempt other ways of resisting.

ACKNOWLEDGEMENTS

To everyone at Penguin Random House and particularly to Marianne Tatepo; thank you for giving me the opportunity of a lifetime, this book would not have seen the light of day without your vision, your guidance and encouragement.

I want to wholeheartedly thank those who have shared words, silences, tears and laughter with me, particularly research participants of my doctoral thesis, upon which *Living While Black* is partly based. Those who have made me feel and think and thus grow as a researcher, as a clinician and as a human. All your voices and experiences and some of my early writing have led me here, to this book.

To 'Black Twitter' to which I owe so much of my intellectual growth and sanity, thank you. You have allowed me to keep thinking when my thinking was under attack, you have given me the intellectual community I needed to grow as a scholar.

A few god-sent people joined me on my journey, they have smoothed the road so I could keep walking along the path of academia. Chief among those are Beverley Stobo, Dr Joanna Wilde, Professor Joanna Bennett and Derek Tuitt, I do not know that I could have kept going or kept hopeful without your support.

The whole Race Reflections community including members, clients and our first ever assistant psychologists Leone Alexander and Charlotte Maxwell for walking alongside us as we took our first steps as a social enterprise and for your support in referencing. To those who have cast their eyes on earlier drafts and provided feedback and encouragement, particularly Martha Crawford, Dr Kate Hammer and Dr Alex Thomson, thank you.

Most importantly, to you Maman. For teaching me moral courage, dignity, integrity, resistance and the value of education.

Finally, to that shy and anxious little Black girl in the banlieue, the hopeless daydreamer who learnt about the injustices of this world way too early, you and I know the odds were stacked against us. But we are here . . . And I am giggling with you. Thank you for fighting all the battles you have had to fight to get us both here.

NOTES AND REFERENCES

Introduction
1. AMA (2020, November 16), *Racism is a threat to public health*, Kevin B. O'Reilly (ama-assn.org)
2. Kinouani, G. (2018, July 24). Reflections on Being a Black Client and a Black Therapist. racereflections.co.uk/reflections-on-setting-up-a-private-practice-part-1-the-gap

Centring Blackness
1. Omi, M. and Winant, H. (1986), *Racial Formation in the United States* (1st ed.), New York: Routledge.
2. Ralph, M. and Singhal, M. (2019). 'Racial capitalism'. *Theory and Society*, 48(6), 851–881.
3. Smedley, A. and Smedley, B. D. (2005) 'Race as Biology Is Fiction, Racism as a Social Problem Is Real: Anthropological and Historical Perspectives on the Social Construction of Race'. *The American Psychologist*, 60(1) pp.16–26.
4. Fernando, S. (2017) *Institutional Racism in Psychiatry and Clinical Psychology: Race Matters in Mental Health*. Cham, Switzerland: Palgrave Macmillan.
5. Schermerhorn, C., 1975. (2015). *The Business of Slavery and the Rise of American Capitalism, 1815–1860*. New Haven, CT: Yale University Press.
6. Allen, T. W. (1994). *The Invention of the White Race*. London: Verso.

Chapter 1 – Being Black
1. Kinouani, G. (2019, April 20), 'Racial trauma, silence and meaning', racereflections.co.uk/racial-trauma-silence-and-meaning.
2. Kinouani, G. (2019, June 10), On school, institutional racism and everyday violence, racereflections.co.uk/on-school-insititutional-racism-&-everyday-violence
3. Hamad, R. (2019). *White Tears/Brown Scars: How White Feminism Betrays Women of Colour* Catapult: Melbourne.

4. Accapadi, M. M. (2007). 'When white women cry: How white women's tears oppress women of color'. *The College Student Affairs Journal,* 26(2), 208.
5. Kinouani, G. (2020). 'Silencing, power, and racial trauma in groups'. *Group Analysis,* 53(2), 145–161.
6. *The Economist* (2020, June 1). 'History is repeated in protests at the death of George Floyd; echoes of 1968'. www.economist.com/united-states/2020/06/01/history-is-repeated-in-protests-at-the-death-of-george-floyd.
7. Steinbuch, Y. and Fitz-Gibbon, J. (2020, June 3). 'Worldwide protests break out over George Floyd's death'. nypost.com/2020/06/03/global-protests-break-out-over-george-floyds-death/.
8. hooks, b., (2001). *All about love: New visions* (1st Perennial ed.). New York: Perennial.

Chapter 2 – Black Minds

1. Department of Health (2005). 'Delivering Race Equality in Mental Health Care: An Action Plan for Reform Inside and Outside Services and the Government's Response to the Independent Inquiry into the Death of David Bennett'.
2. Bhui, K., Ullrich, S., Kallis, C. and Coid, J.W. (2015). 'Criminal justice pathways to psychiatric care for psychosis'. *British Journal of Psychiatry,* 207, 523–9.
3. Nazroo, J. Y., Bhui, K. S. and Rhodes, J. (2019). 'Where next for understanding race/ethnic inequalities in severe mental illness? Structural, interpersonal, and institutional racism'. *Sociology of Health & Illness,* 42(2), 262–276. doi.org/10.1111/1467-9566.13001.
4. Das-Munshi, J., Bhugra, D. and Crawford, M. J. (2018). 'Ethnic minority inequalities in access to treatments for schizophrenia and schizoaffective disorders: findings from a nationally representative cross-sectional study'. *BMC Medicine,* 16, 55.
5. Keating, F. (2007). 'African and Caribbean Men and Mental Health, Better Health Briefing 5'. London: Race Equality Foundation.
6. Lo, C. C., Cheng, T. C. and Howell, R. J. (2014). 'Access to and utilization of health services as pathway to racial disparities in serious mental illness'. *Community Mental Health Journal,* 50(3), 251–257.
7. De Luca, S. M., Blosnich, J. R., Hentschel, E. A., King, E. and Amen, S. (2016). 'Mental health care utilization: How race, ethnicity and veteran status are associated with seeking help'. *Community Mental Health Journal,* 52(2), 174–179.
8. Ward, E. and Mengesha, M. (2013). 'Depression in African American men: A review of what we know and where we need to go from here'. *American Journal of Orthopsychiatry,* 83(2–3), 386–397. doi:10.1111/ajop.12015.
9. Gara, M. A., Minksky, S., Silverstein, S. M., Miskimen, T., and Strakowski, S. M. 'A Naturalistic Study of Racial Disparities in Diagnoses at an Outpatient Behavioral Health Clinic'. *Psychiatric Services,* 2019; 70 (2): 130.
10. Eack S. M., Bahorik A. L., Newhill C. E., Neighbors H. W. and Davis L. E. 'Interviewer-perceived honesty as a mediator of racial disparities in the diagnosis of schizophrenia'. *Psychiatr Serv.* 2012; 63:875–880.

11. Schwartz, R. and Blankenship, M. (2014) 'Racial disparities in psychotic disorder diagnosis: A review of empirical literature'. *World J Psychiatry*. 22; 4(4): 133–140.

12. Halvorsrud, K., Nazroo, J., Otis, M., Brown Hajdukova, E. and Bhui, K. (2019). 'Ethnic inequalities in the incidence of diagnosis of severe mental illness in England: a systematic review and new meta-analyses for non-affective and affective psychoses'. *Social Psychiatry and Psychiatric Epidemiology*. doi.org/10.1007/s00127-019-01758-y

13. Couto, C., Barreto, S. and Rolim Neto, M. L. (2018). 'Suicide in Black children'. *International Journal of Social Psychiatry*, 64(5), 506–508. doi:10.1177/0020764018770477

14. SAMHSA. (2020). 'Alarming suicide trends in African American children: An urgent issue'. Rockville: Newstex.

15. Tolmac, J. and Hodes, M. (2004). 'Ethnic variation among adolescent psychiatric in-patients with psychotic disorders'. *British Journal of Psychiatry*, 184(5), 428–431.

16. The Independent Inquiry set up under HSG (94)27 (2003, December). image.guardian.co.uk/sys-files/Society/documents/2004/02/12/Bennett.pdf

17. Norton-Taylor, R. (1999). *The Colour of Justice: Based on the Transcripts of the Stephen Lawrence Inquiry.* London: Oberon Books.

18. Bor, J., Venkataramani, A. S., Williams, D. R. and Tsai, A. C. (2018). 'Police killings and their spillover effects on the mental health of Black Americans: A population-based, quasi-experimental study'. *The Lancet (British Edition)*, 392(10144), 302–310

19. Frankham, E. (2018, Spring). 'Mental illness affects police fatal shootings'. https://journals.sagepub.com/doi/pdf/10.1177/1536504218776970

20. Fernando, S. (2017). *Institutional Racism in Psychiatry and Clinical Psychology: Race Matters in Mental Health.* Cham, Switzerland: Palgrave Macmillan.

21. Bhui, K., Halvorsrud, K., Rhodes, J., Nazroo & Francis, J. (2018). The impact of racism on mental health: Briefing paper. London: The Synergi Collaborative Centre.

22. Harnett, N. G. (2020). 'Neurobiological consequences of racial disparities and environmental risks: a critical gap in understanding psychiatric disorders'. *Neuropsychopharmacology*, 45, 1247–50.

23. Karlsen, S., Nazroo, J. Y., McKenzie, K., Bhui, K. S. and Weich, S. (2005). 'Racism, psychosis, and common mental health disorder among ethnic minority groups in England'. *Psychological Medicine*, 35, 1795–1803.

24. APA (2020). APA Dictionary of Psychology. dictionary.apa.org/trauma.

25. APA (2013). American Psychiatric Association, & American Psychiatric Association. Task Force on DSM-V. (2013). *Diagnostic and statistical manual of mental disorders: DSM-IV-TR* (5th, text revision. ed.). Washington, DC: American Psychiatric Association.

26. Kirkinis, K., Pieterse, A. L., Martin, C., Agiliga A. and Brownell, A. (2018). 'Racism, racial discrimination, and trauma: a systematic review of the social science literature'. *Ethnicity & Health*, 1–21.

27. Carter, R. T. (2006, December 1). www.psychiatrictimes.com/view/race-based-traumatic-stress

28. Harrell, S. P. (2000). 'A Multidimensional Conceptualization of Racism-Related Stress: Implications for the Wellbeing of People of Color'. *American Journal of Orthopsychiatry*, 70(1), 42–57.

29. Alexander, J. C., 1947. (2004). *Cultural Trauma and Collective Identity* (1st ed.). Berkeley, Calif: University of California Press.

30. Knight, R. P. (1940). 'Introjection, projection, and identification'. *The Psychoanalytic Quarterly*, 9(3), 334–341.

31. Sullivan, S. (2013). 'Inheriting Racist Disparities in Health: Epigenetics and the Transgenerational Effects of White Racism'. *Critical Philosophy of Race*, 1(2), 190–218.

32. Avramova, Z. (2015). 'Transcriptional "memory" of a stress: Transient chromatin and memory (epigenetic) marks at stress-response genes'. *The Plant Journal: For Cell and Molecular Biology*, 83(1), 149–159.

33. Mangassarian, S. L. (2016). '100 years of trauma: the Armenian genocide and intergenerational cultural trauma'. *Journal of Aggression, Maltreatment and Trauma*, 25, 371–381.

34. Münyas B. (2008). 'Genocide in the minds of Cambodian youth: transmitting (hi)stories of genocide to second and third generations in Cambodia'. *Journal of Genocide Research*, 10(3), 413–439.

35. Salberg, J. (2019). 'When trauma tears the fabric of attachment: Discussion of "the intergenerational transmission of holocaust trauma: A psychoanalytic theory revisited"'. *The Psychoanalytic Quarterly*, 88(3), 563–582.

36. Sharpley, M. S., Hutchinson, G., Murray, R. M. and McKenzie, K. (2001). 'Understanding the excess of psychosis among the African-Caribbean population in England: Review of current hypotheses'. *The British Journal of Psychiatry*, 178(40), s60–s68.

37. Van der Kolk, Bessel A., (2015). *The Body Keeps the Score: Mind, Brain and Body in the Transformation of Trauma*. New York: Penguin

38. Pal, R. and Elbers, J. (2018). 'Neuroplasticity: The other side of the coin'. *Paediatric Neurology*, 84, 3–4.

39. Gilbert, P. (2014). 'The origins and nature of compassion focused therapy'. *British Journal of Clinical Psychology*, 53(1), 6–41.

40. Alkozei, A., Smith, R. and Killgore, W. D. S. (2017;2018;). 'Gratitude and subjective wellbeing: A proposal of two causal frameworks'. *Journal of Happiness Studies*, 19(5), 1519–1542.

Chapter 3 – Black Shame

1. Crenshaw, K. W. (1989). 'Demarginalizing the intersection of race and sex: a Black feminist critique of anti-discrimination doctrine, feminist theory, and anti-racist politics'. *The University of Chicago Legal Forum*, 140, 139–167

2. Watson, L. B., DeBlaere, C., Langrehr, K. J., Zelaya, D. G. and Flores, M. J. (2016). 'The influence of multiple oppressions on women of color's experiences with insidious trauma'. *Journal Of Counselling Psychology*, 63 (6), 656–667. doi:10.1037/cou00001

3. Fanon, F. (1970). *Black Skin, White Masks*. London: Paladin.

4. Kinouani, G (2019, July 18). 'Internalised racism and the colour of power'. racereflections.co.uk/internalised-racism-the-colour-of-power

5. Khan, A. (2017, March 15). 'SCIENCE FILE: Black men's plight as "superhuman"; bias that minority males are bigger, more menacing than white men may play role in police shootings'. *The Los Angeles*.

6. Kinouani, G. (2015, October 18) 'Shame and Marginalisation: An Intersubjective Formulation Model'. racereflections.co.uk/shame-and-marginalisation-an-intersubjective-formulation-model

7. Pickersgill, M. D. (2014). 'Debating DSM-5: diagnosis and the sociology of critique'. *Journal of Medical Ethics*, 40, 521–525.

8. Kinouani, G. (2017, June 1). 'Culturally Biased CBT, part 2: Injustice and depression'. racereflections.co.uk/culturally-biased-therapy-part-2-injustice-and-depression

9. Kinouani, G. (2020, November 1). 'Epistemic Homelessness'. racereflections.co.uk/epistemic-homelessness

10. Pierce, C. (1970). 'Offensive mechanisms'. In Barbour F (ed.). *In the Black Seventies*. Boston, MA: Porter Sargent.

11. Bowlby, J. (1969). *Attachment and Loss, Volume I: Attachment*. New York: Basic Books.

12. Zeanah, C. H., Berlin, L. J. and Boris, N. W. (2011). 'Practitioner Review: Clinical applications of attachment theory and research for infants and young children'. *Journal of Child Psychology and Psychiatry*, 52(8), 819–833.

13. Hidalgo, M. C. and Hernandez, B. (2001). 'Place Attachment: Conceptual and Empirical Questions'. *Journal of Environmental Psychology*, 21(3), 273–281.

14. Kinouani, G. (2020, May 21). 'On home, places, and loss'. racereflections.co.uk/on-attachment-place-and-otherness

15. Yeo, C. (2018, May 1). 'Free Movement. Briefing: what is the hostile environment, where does it come from, who does it affect?' www.free-movement.org.uk/briefing-what-is-the-hostile-environment-where-does-it-come-from-who-does-it-affect

16. Rawlinson, K. (2018, November 12). 'Windrush: 11 people wrongly deported from UK have died – Javid'. www.theguardian.com/uk-news/2018/nov/12/windrush-11-people-wrongly-deported-from-uk-have-died-sajid-javid

17. Government website (2019, June 10). www.gov.uk/government/news/home-secretary-apologises-to-members-of-windrush-generation

18. Ritsner, M. and Ponizovsky, A. (1999). 'Psychological distress through immigration: The two-phase temporal pattern?'. *International Journal of Social Psychiatry*, 45(2), 125–139.

19. Vivero, V. and Jenkins, R. (1999). 'Existential hazards of the multicultural individual: Defining and understanding "cultural homelessness"'. *Cultural Diversity & Ethnic Minority Psychology*, pp.6–26.

Chapter 4 – Black Bodies

1. Kinouani, G. (2020, September 21). 'Whiteness, Sovereignty and the Body'. racereflections.co.uk/whiteness-sovereignty-and-the-body

2. Kellaway, K. (2015, December 27). Interview Claudia Rankine: 'Blackness in the white imagination has nothing to do with Black people'. www.theguardian.com/books/2015/dec/27/claudia-rankine-poet-citizen-american-lyric-feature

3. Sanburn, J. (2014, November 25). 'All the Ways Darren Wilson Described Being Afraid of Michael Brown'. time.com/3605346/darren-wilson-michael-brown-demon

4. Fanon, F. (1970). *Black Skin, White Masks*. London: Paladin.

5. Bateman, A. and Holmes, J. (1995). *Introduction to Psychoanalysis: Contemporary Theory and Practice*. London: Routledge.

6. Shohat, E. (1992) 'Notes on the "Post-Colonial".' *Social text*, 31–32(31/32) pp.99–113.

7. Feinberg, J. (1989). *The Moral Limits of the Criminal Law Volume 3: Harm to Self*. New York: Oxford University Press.

8. Kinouani, G. (2019, January 26). 'Brexit, the body and politics of the splitting'. racereflections.co.uk/brexit-the-body-politics-of-splitting

9. Stobo, B. (2005). 'Location of disturbance with a focus on race, difference and culture'. Birkbeck College, UK.

10. Ahmed, S. (2017). *Living a Feminist Life*. Durham, North Carolina; London, England: Duke University Press Books.

11. Eisenman, R. (1965). 'Scapegoating and Social Control'. *The Journal of Psychology*, 61(2) pp.203–209.

12. Campbell, C. (2011). *Scapegoat: A History of Blaming Other People*. London; New York: Duckworth Overlook.

13 Sandler, J. (1988). 'The Concept of Projective Identification'. In J. Sandler, (Eds). *Projection, Identification, Projective Identification*. London: Karmac Books Ltd.

14. Magruder, K. M., McLaughlin, K. A. and Elmore Borbon, D. L. (2017). 'Trauma is a public health issue'. *European Journal of Psychotraumatology*, 8(1) pp.1375338-1375339.

15. Range, B., Gutierrez, D., Gamboni, C., Hough, N. A. and Wojciak, A. (2018) 'Mass Trauma in the African American Community: Using Multiculturalism to Build Resilient Systems'. *Contemporary Family Therapy*, 40(3) pp.284–298.

16 Afari, N., Ahumada, S. M., Wright, L. J., Mostoufi, S., Golnari, G., Reis, V. and Cuneo, J. G. (2014) 'Psychological trauma and functional somatic syndromes: a systematic review and meta-analysis'. *Psychosomatic Medicine*, 76(1) pp.2–11.14. Heenan, A., Greenman, P.

17 Jackson, J. (2015). 'Racism and cardiovascular disease: Implications for practice'. *Canadian Journal of Cardiology*, 31(10), S314–S314.

18 Bell, C., Kerr, J. and Young, J. (2019). 'Associations between obesity, obesogenic environments, and structural racism vary by county-level racial composition'. *International Journal of Environmental Research and Public Health*, 16(5), 861.

19 Arigo, D., Juth, V., Trief, P., Wallston, K., Ulbrecht, J. and Smyth, J. M. (2020). 'Unique relations between post-traumatic stress disorder symptoms and patient functioning in type 2 diabetes'. *Journal of health psychology*, 25(5) pp.652–664.

20 Bayley-Veloso, R., Szabo, Y. Z., Cash, E., Zimmaro, L., Siwik, C., Kloecker, G., Salmon, P., van der Gryp, K., et al. (2020). 'The association between history of traumatic events and health-related quality of life among lung cancer patients'. *Journal of Psychosocial Oncology*, 38(5) pp.627–634.

21. American Cancer Society. (2019). *Cancer Facts and Figures for African Americans 2019–2021*. Atlanta: American Cancer Society.

22. Chinegwundoh, F. (2018, June 12). 'Time to talk about the prostate cancer risk in Black men and what we can do about it'. www.england. nhs.uk/blog/time-to-talk,about-the-prostate-cancer-risk-in-Black-men-and-what-we-can-do-about-it

23 Chae, D. H., Wang, Y., Martz, C. D., Slopen et al. (2020). 'The Coronary Artery Risk Development in Young Adults (CARDIA) Study'. *Health Psychol:* 39(3):209–219.

24 Thames, A. D., Irwin, M. R., Breen, E. C. and Cole. S. W. (2019). 'Experienced discrimination and racial differences in leukocyte gene expression'. *Psychoneuroendocrinology*, 106(277) doi: 10.1016/j.psyneuen.2019.04.016

25 Lee, D. B., Kim, E. S. and Neblett, E. W., Jr. (2017). 'The link between discrimination and telomere length in African American adults'. *Health Psychology*, 36(5), 458–467.

26 Segerstrom, S., Miller, G., (2006). 'Psychological stress and the human immune system: A meta-analytic study of 30 years inquiry'. *Psychological Bulletin*, 130(4), 601–630.

27 Jie Yong, S. (2020, June 10). 'How Racism Provokes Cellular Ageing, Stress, and Inflammation. medium.com/the-faculty/how-racism-provokes-cellular-ageing-stress-and-inflammation-17afece56def

28 University of Southern California. (2019, May 31). 'Racism has a toxic effect: Study may explain how racial discrimination raises the risks of disease among African Americans'. *ScienceDaily*.

29. Barber, S. (2020). 'Death by racism'. *The Lancet Infectious Diseases*, 20(8), 903–903.

30. Liu, S. R. and Modir, S. (2020). 'The Outbreak That Was Always Here: Racial Trauma in the Context of COVID-19 and Implications for Mental Health Providers'. *Psychological Trauma*, 12(5) pp.439–442.

31. Powell, W., Richmond, J., Mohottige, D., Yen, I., Joslyn, A. and Corbie-Smith, G. (2019). 'Medical Mistrust, Racism, and Delays in Preventive Health Screening Among African American Men'. *Behavioral Medicine*, 45(2), 102.

32. Hong, Y., Tauscher, J. and Cardel, M. (2018). 'Distrust in health care and cultural factors are associated with uptake of colorectal cancer screening in hispanic and asian americans'. *Cancer*, 124(2), 335–345.

33. Mingucci, G. (2018). 'René Descartes' Parricide: The Challenge of Cartesian Philosophy of Nature and Philosophy of Mind to Aristotle's Authorship'. *Societies şi politică*, 12(1).

34. Kinouani, G. (2019, January 19). 'Brexit, the body & the politics of splitting'. racereflections.co.uk/brexit-the-body-politics-of-splitting

Chapter 5 – Raising Black Children

1. Kinouani, G. (2019). 'On school, institutional racism and everyday violence'. Race Reflections.

2. Hill, S. A. (1999). *African American Children: Socialization and Development in Families*. SAGE Publications.

3. Burt, C. H., Simons, R. L. and Gibbons, F. X. (2012). 'Racial Discrimination, Ethnic-Racial Socialization, and Crime: A Micro-sociological Model of Risk and Resilience'. *American Sociological Review*, 77(4) pp. 648–677.

4. Hurst, G. (2020, January 02). 'Primary schools suspend 40% more pupils for racist behaviour'. www.thetimes.co.uk/article/primary-schools-suspend-40-more-pupils-for-racist-behaviour-rrwh66mpt

5. McGrew., K. (2016). 'The Dangers of Pipeline Thinking: How the School-To-Prison Pipeline Metaphor Squeezes Out Complexity'. *Educational Theory*. 66 (3): 341–367

6. The Stephen Lawrence Enquiry. (1999, February) 'Report of an inquiry by Sir William Macpherson of Cluny'. assets.publishing.service.gov.uk/government/uploads/system/uploads/attachment_data/file/277111/4262.pdf

7. Levs, J. (2017, July 27). 'No, Most Black Kids Are Not Fatherless'. *HuffPost*

8. Geary. D. (2015). *Beyond Civil Rights: The Moynihan Report and Its Legacy*. Pennsylvania: University of Pennsylvania Press.

9. McAdoo, H. P. (1997). *Black Families*. 3rd ed., London; SAGE Publishing.

10. Bernard, C., & Harris, P. (2016). *Safeguarding Black Children: Good practice in child protection*. London; Philadelphia; Jessica Kingsley Publishers.

11. BBC News. (2012, October 3) 'David Lammy MP says absent fathers "key cause of knife crime"'. www.bbc.co.uk/news/uk-england-london-19815831, *BBC News*.

12. Kessler, R. C., McLaughlin, K. A., Green, J. G., Gruber, M. J., Sampson, N. A., Zaslavsky, A. M., Aguilar-Gaxiola, S., Alhamzawi, A. O., et al. (2010). 'Childhood adversities and adult psychopathology in the WHO World Mental Health Surveys'. *British Journal of Psychiatry*, 197(5) pp.378–385.

13. Norrick, N. R. (2019). 'Collaborative Remembering in Conversational Narration'. *Topics in Cognitive Science*, 11(4) pp.733–751.

14. Ritter, M. (2014). 'Silence as the voice of trauma'. *The American Journal of Psychoanalysis*, 74(2) p.176.

15. Lopez, G. (2026, August 8). 'Black parents describe "The Talk" they give to their children about the police'. www.vox.com/2016/8/8/12401792/police-Black-parents-the-talk

16. Feay, S. (2020, June 19). 'The school that tried to end racism, Channel 4–can bias be reprogrammed?'. www.ft.com/content/34d84740-af16-11ea-a4b6-31f1eedf762e

17. Office for National Statistics. (2011). '2011 Census analysis: International Migration'. www.ons.gov.uk/peoplepopulationandcommunity/populationandmigration/internationalmigration

18. McCarthy, A., 1971, and Coleborne, C. (2012). *Migration, Ethnicity, and Mental Health: International Perspectives, 1840–2010*. New York: Routledge.

19. Ingleby, D. (2005). *Forced Migration and Mental Health: Rethinking the Care of Refugees and Displaced Persons*. New York: Springer.

20. Anderson, M. and Lopez, G. (2018, January 24). 'Key facts about Black immigrants in the U.S.' www.pewresearch.org/fact-tank/2018/01/24/key-facts-about-Black-immigrants-in-the-u-s

21. Feltz, R. (2006, October 16). 'Black Migrants more likely to be deported'. www.theguardian.com/us-news/2016/oct/03/Black-immigrants-us-deportation-rates-criminal-convictions

22. Kinouani, G. (In press). 'Death by a thousand cuts: A phenomenological investigation of people of African descent in the UK'.

23. Mooney, C. G. (2010; 2009). *Theories of Attachment: An Introduction to Bowlby, Ainsworth, Gerber, Brazelton, Kennell, and Klaus* (1st ed.). St. Paul, MN: Redleaf Press.

24. Ainsworth, M. D. S., Blehar, M., Waters, E. and Wall, S. N. (2015). *Patterns of attachment: A Psychological Study of the Strange Situation* (Classic ed.). New York, NY: Psychology Press/Taylor & Francis Group.

25. Brewster, F. (2019). *Archetypal Grief: Slavery's Legacy of Intergenerational Child Loss*. Abingdon, Oxon; New York, NY: Routledge.

26. Speight, S. L. (2007). 'Internalized racism: One more piece of the puzzle'. *The Counselling Psychologist*, 35(1), 126–34.

27. Du Bois, W. E. B. (William Edward Burghardt), 1868–1963 and Alexander, S. L. (2018). *The Souls of Black Folk: Essays and sketches*. Amherst: UMass Amherst Libraries; Boston: University of Massachusetts Press.

28. Distel, L. M. L., Egbert, A. H., Bohnert, A. M. and Santiago, C. D. (2019). 'Chronic stress and food insecurity: Examining key environmental family factors related to body mass index among low-income Mexican-origin youth'. *Family & Community Health*, 42(3), 213–220. 29.

29. Sue, D. W. (2016). *Race Talk and the Conspiracy of Silence: Understanding and Facilitating Difficult Dialogues on Race*. London: John Wiley & Sons, Incorporated.

30. Osborne, K. R., Caughy, M. O., Oshri, A., Smith, E. P. and Owen, M. T. (2020). 'Racism and preparation for bias within African American families'. *Cultural Diversity & Ethnic Minority Psychology*, doi:10.1037/cdp0000339

31. Graham, J. R., West, L. M. and Roemer, L. (2012;2013). 'The experience of racism and anxiety symptoms in an African-American sample: Moderating effects of trait mindfulness'. *Mindfulness*, 4(4), 332–341.

32. Goff, P. A., Jackson, M. C., Di Leone, Brooke Allison Lewis, Culotta, C. M. and DiTomasso, N. A. (2014). 'The essence of innocence: Consequences of dehumanizing Black children'. *Journal of Personality and Social Psychology*, 106(4), 526–545.

33. Haylock, S., Boshari, T., Alexander, E. C., Kumar, A., Manikam, L., & Pinder, R. (2020). 'Risk factors associated with knife-crime in united kingdom among young people aged 10–24 years: A systematic review'. *BMC Public Health*, 20(1), 1–1451.

Chapter 6 – Working While Black

1. Newkirk, P. (2019). 'Diversity Has Become a Booming Business. So Where Are the Results?'. time.com/5696943/diversity-business

2. Alexander, C., and Arday, J. (2015). 'Aiming Higher: Race, Inequality and Diversity in the Academy'. London: Runnymede Trust. www.runnymedetrust.org/uploads/Aiming%20Higher.pdf

3. HESA. (2018). Student record 2017–18. www.hesa.ac.uk/collection/c17051

4. Jameel, M. and Yerardi, J. (2019, February 29). 'Workplace discrimination is illegal. But our data shows it is still a huge problem'. www.vox.com/policy-and-politics/2019/2/28/18241973/workplace-discrimination-cpi-investigation-eeoc

5. Awori, R. (2018, December 10). 'Victory for Lettia McNickle: I am not my hair'. montrealcommunitycontact.com/lettias-hairstyle-a-problem-at-madisons

6. Byrd, A. D. and Tharps, L. L. (2002). *Hair Story: Untangling the Roots of Black Hair in America*. London: St Martin's Press.

7. Dabiri, E. (2019). *Don't Touch My Hair*. London: Penguin.

8. Krivkovich, A., Nadeau, M., Robinson, K., Robinson, N., Starikova, I. and Yee, L. (2018). 'Women in the Workplace Report'. www.mckinsey.com/featured-insights/diversity-and-inclusion/women-in-the-workplace#

9. Bhopal, K. (2018). *White Privilege: The Myth of a Post-racial Society*. Bristol: Policy Press.

10. Spencer, S. J., Steele, C. M. and Quinn, D. M. (1999). 'Stereotype Threat and Women's Math Performance'. *Journal of Experimental Social Psychology*, 35(1), 4–28.

11. Steele, C. (2003). 'Stereotype-threat and African American Student Achievement'. In D. B. Grusky & S. Szelenyi. (2011). *The Inequality Reader: Contemporary and Foundational Readings in Race, Class, and Gender*. Routledge.

12. Steele, C. M. and Aronson, J. (1998). 'Stereotype threat and the test performance of academically successful African Americans'. In C. Jencks & M. Phillips (Eds.), *The Black–White test score gap* (pp. 401–427). Brookings Institution Press.

13. Bratter, J. L., Rowley, K. J. and Chukhray, I. (2016). 'Does a Self-Affirmation Intervention Reduce Stereotype Threat in Black and Hispanic High Schools?'. *Race and Social Problems*, 8, 340–356.

14. Bullock, J., Lockspeiser, T., del Pino-Jones, A., Richards, Regina P., Teherani, A. and Hauer, K. E. (2020). 'They Do not See a Lot of People My Color: A Mixed Methods Study of Racial/Ethnic Stereotype Threat Among Medical Students on Core Clerkships'. *Academic Medicine*. doi: 10.1097/ACM.0000000000003628

15. Nadler, D. R. and Komarraju, M. (2016). 'Negating Stereotype Threat: Autonomy Support and Academic Identification Boost Performance of African American College Students'. *Journal of College Student Development*, 57(6), 667–679. doi:10.1353/csd.2016.0039.

16. Clance, P. R., and Imes, S. A. (1978). 'The imposter phenomenon in high achieving women: Dynamics and therapeutic intervention'. *Psychotherapy: Theory, Research & Practice*, 15(3), 241–247. doi.org/10.1037/h0086006

17. Shilliam, R. (2015). 'Black Academia: The Doors Have Been Opened but the Architecture Remains the Same'. In C. Alexander and J. Arday (2015). *Aiming Higher: Race, Inequality and Diversity in the Academy*. Runnymede Trust.

18. Sellers, S. L., Neighbors, H. W. and Bonham, V. L. (2011). 'Goal-striving stress and the mental health of college-educated Black american men: The protective effects of system-blame'. *American Journal of Orthopsychiatry*, 81(4), 507–518.

19. James, S. A., Keenan, N. L., Strogatz, D. S., Browning, S. R. and Garrett, J. M. (1992). 'Socioeconomic status, John Henryism, and blood pressure in Black adults'. The Pitt County Study. *American Journal of Epidemiology*. 135 (1): 59–67.

Chapter 7 – Black Love

1. Clark, K. B., and Clark, M. P. (1947). 'Racial identification and preferences in negro children'. *Readings in Social Psychology*. New York: Holt.
2. Dickey-Bryant, L., Lautenschlager, G. J., Mendoza, J. L. and Abrahams, N. (1986). 'Facial attractiveness and its relation to occupational success'. *Journal of Applied Psychology*, 71(1), 16–19.
3. Chito Childs, E. (2005). 'Looking behind the stereotypes of the "Angry Black Woman"'. *Gender & Society*, 19(4), 544–561.
4. Bland, L. (2017). 'Interracial Relationships and the "Brown Baby Question": Black GIs, White British Women, and Their Mixed-Race Offspring in World War II'. *Journal of the History of Sexuality*, 26(3) pp. 424–453.
5. Office for National Statistics. (2011). 2011 Census analysis: 'What does the 2011 Census tell us about Inter-ethnic Relationships?'. www.ons.gov.uk
6. Pew Research Center. (2017). 'Trends and Patterns in Intermarriage'. www.pewsocialtrends.org/2017/05/18/1-trends-and-patterns-in-intermarriage
7. Cruz, B. C. and Berson, M. J. (2001). 'The American Melting Pot? Miscegenation Laws in the United States'. *OAH Magazine of History*, 15(4), 80–84. www.jstor.org/stable/25163474.
8. Hollinger, D. A. (2005). 'The one drop rule & the one hate rule'. *Daedalus*, 134(1), 18–28.
9. Nayabola, N. (2011). 'Satoshi Kanazawa's racist nonsense should not be tolerated'. www.theguardian.com/commentisfree/2011/may/18/satoshi-kanazawa-Black-women-psychology-today.
10. Jackson, L. (2019). *White Negroes: When Cornrows Were in Vogue . . . and Other Thoughts on Cultural Appropriation*. Beacon Press.
11. Collins, P. H. (2000). *Black Feminist Thought: Knowledge, Consciousness, and the Politics of Empowerment*. Routledge.
12. Dabiri, E. (2013). 'Who stole all the Black women from Britain?'. mediadiversified.org/2013/11/05/who-stole-all-the-Black-women-from-britain
13. Dabiri, E. (2019). *Don't Touch My Hair*. Penguin Random House UK.
14. Moynihan, D. P. (1965). *The Negro Family: The Case for National Action*. Washington, D.C., Office of Policy Planning and Research, US Department of Labour.
15. Washington, J. (2010). 'Blacks struggle with 72 percent unwed mothers' rate'. NBC News. www.nbcnews.com/id/wbna39993685#.URXHo80hclk
16. Brown, T. and Patterson, E. (2016). 'Wounds from Incarceration that Never Heal'. *The New Republic*. newrepublic.com/article/134712/wounds-incarceration-never-heal
17. Williams, H. A. (n.d.). 'How Slavery Affected African American Families'. nationalhumanitiescenter.org/tserve/freedom/1609–1865/essays/aafamilies.htm
18. Fanon, F. (1970). *Black Skin, White Masks*. London: Paladin.
19. Appelbaum, N. (1999). 'Whitening the Region: Caucano Mediation and "Antioqueño Colonization" in Nineteenth Century Colombia'. *Hispanic American Historical Review*, 79(4), 631–667. doi: 10.1215/00182168-79.4.631
20. Jones, B. E. and Hill, M. J. (1996). 'African American lesbians, gay men, and bisexuals'. In Cabaj, R. P., Stein, T. S. and Terry, S. (1996). *Textbook*

of homosexuality and mental health, 549–561. Washington, DC: American Psychiatric Association.

21. M'Baye, B. (2013). 'The Origins of Senegalese Homophobia: Discourses on Homosexuals and Transgender People in Colonial and Postcolonial Senegal'. *African Studies Review*, 56(2), 109–128.

22. Foster, T. A. (2011). 'The Sexual Abuse of Black Men under American Slavery'. *Journal of the History of Sexuality*, 20(3), 445–464.

23. Dudley, R. G. (2013). 'Being Black and Lesbian, Gay, Bisexual or Transgender'. *Journal of Gay & Lesbian Mental Health*, 17(2), 183–195.

Chapter 8 – Black Resistance

1. Southern Poverty Law Center. (n.d.). 'Civil Rights Martyrs'. www.splcenter.org/what-we-do/civil-rights-memorial/civil-rights-martyrs

2. Fernando, S. (2017). *Institutional Racism in Clinical Psychology and Psychiatry: Race Matters in Mental Health*. London: Palgrave MacMillan.

3. McKenzie, K. and Bhui, K. (2007). 'Institutional racism in mental health care'. *British Medical Journal*, 334(7595), 649–650. doi: 10.1136/bmj.39163.395972.80.

4. Polanco-Roman, L., Danies, A., & Anglin, D. M. (2016). 'Racial discrimination as race-based trauma, coping strategies, and dissociative symptoms among emerging adults'. *Psychological Trauma: Theory, Research, Practice and Policy*, 8 (5), 609–617. doi:10.1037/tra0000125

5. Raymond, C. (2014). *Witnessing Sadism in Texts of the American South: Women, Specularity, and the Poetics of Subjectivity*. Surrey: Ashgate Publishing.

6. Morrison, T. (1975). 'Portland State, "Black Studies Center public dialogue. Pt. 2" May 30, 1975'. soundcloud.com/portland-state-library/portland-state-Black-studies-1?mc_cid=7a27cfd978&mc_eid=e2efbcffa9

7. Eddo-Lodge, R. (2017). *Why I'm No Longer Talking to White People About Race*. London: Bloomsbury Publishing.

8. Association for Dance Movement Psychotherapy. (2020). Research and Publications. admp.org.uk

9. Gabriel, D. (2007). *Layers of Blackness: Colourism in the African Diaspora*. London: Imani Media.

10. Sarvan, C. (2000). 'The Term "Racism" and Discourse'. *The Journal of Commonwealth Literature*, 129–137.

11. Middleton, R. T. (2008). 'Institutions, inculcation, and Black racial identity: pigmentocracy vs. the rule of hypodescent'. *Social Identities*, 14(5), 567–585.

12. Angelou, M. (1986). *And Still I Rise*. London: Virago Press.

13. Glick, E. F. (2003) 'Harlem's Queer Dandy: African-American Modernism And The Artifice Of Blackness.' *Modern Fiction Studies*, 49(3) pp.414–442.

14. Stone, M.-L. (2020). 'Congolese Dandies: Meet the stylish men and women of Brazzaville-in pictures'. *The Guardian*.

15. hooks, b. (1992). *Black Looks: Race and Representation*. Boston: South End Press.

16. Kinouani, G. (2016, January 17). 'Beauty as resistance: On marginalisation, style & self-love'. racereflections.co.uk/beauty-as-resistance-on-marginalisation-style-self-love
17. Scott, S. C. (2017). 'Black Excellence: Fostering Intellectual Curiosity in Minority Honors Students at a Predominantly White Research Institution'. *Journal of the National Collegiate Honors Council*, 18(1).
18. Lozenski, B. D. (2017). 'Beyond Mediocrity: The Dialectics of Crisis in the Continuing Miseducation of Black Youth'. *Harvard Educational Review*, 87(2), 161–185.
19. Kinouani, G. (2015, October 18). racereflections.co.uk/shame-and-marginalisation-an-intersubjective-formulation-model
20. Fanon, F. (1970). *Black Skin, White Masks*. London: Paladin.
21. Johnson, A. J. and Wakefield, J. (2020). 'Examining associations between racism, internalized shame, and self-esteem among African Americans'. *Cogent Psychology*, 7(1).
22. Berry, J. W. (2006). 'Acculturation: A Conceptual Overview'. In M. H. Bornstein and L. R Cote (Eds.), *Acculturation and parent–child relationships: Measurement and development* (pp.13–30). Lawrence Erlbaum Associates Publishers.
23. Jomo Kenyatta, reported in Walker, J. F. (2004) *A Certain Curve of Horn: The Hundred-Year Quest for the Giant Sable Antelope of Angola* (2004), p.144. London: Grove Press.
(it must be noted that the origin of the quote remains contested)
24. Lugo, L. and Cooperman, A. (2010). 'Tolerance and tension: Islam and Christianity in sub-Saharan Africa', Pew Research Center, Washington, DC.
25. Ebersohl, C. (Fall, 2017). 'Religion and Resistance in Enslaved Communities'. civilwar.vt.edu/religion-and-resistance-in-enslaved-communities
26. Nweke, K. C. and Okpaleke, I. P. (2019). 'The re-emergence of African spiritualities: Prospects and challenges'. *Transformation (Exeter)*, 36(4), 246–265.
27. Royal College of Psychiatrists. (2013). 'Recommendations for psychiatrists on spirituality and religion: Position Statement'. www.rcpsych.ac.uk/pdf/ps03_2013.pdf
28. Kinouani, G. (2019, August 11). 'Finding Black Joy Amidst Black Pain'. racereflections.co.uk/finding-Black-joy-amidst-Black-pain
29. Raymond, C. (2014). *Witnessing Sadism in Texts of the American South: Women, Specularity, and the Poetics of Subjectivity*. Surrey: Ashgate Publishing.
30. Du Bois, W. E. B. (1903). *The Souls of Black Folk*. London: New Dover Publishers.
31. Freire, P. (1970). 'Cultural Action and Conscientization'. *Harvard Educational Review*, 4(3), 452–477.
32. Seligman, M. E. P. (1972). 'Learned Helplessness'. *Annual Review of Medicine*, 23, 407–412.
33. Neff, K. (n.d.) 'Definition of Self-Compassion' (suggest replacement as this is the page that the link takes me to). self-compassion.org/the-three-elements-of-self-compassion-2

34. Neff, K. (2003). 'Self-Compassion: An Alternative Conceptualization of a Healthy Attitude Toward Oneself'. *Self and Identity*, 2(2), 85–101. doi. org/10.1080/15298860309032

35. Wilson, D. (2012). 'Competency, connectedness, and consciousness'. In V. D. Woods, N. J. King, S. M. Hanna and C. Murray (Ed.) 'We ain't crazy! Just coping with a crazy system: Pathways into the Black population for eliminating mental health disparities'. *California Reducing Disparities Project (CRDP) African American Report*, 159–161

INDEX

Page numbers in **bold** show a glossary entry

INDEX